FROM BROKEN
to
BUTTERFLY

by Nina Pajonas

From Broken to Butterfly

Trilogy Christian Publishers

A Wholly Owned Subsidiary of Trinity Broadcasting Network

2442 Michelle Drive, Tustin, CA 92780

Copyright © 2024 by Nina Pajonas

Scripture quotations marked NIV are taken from the Holy Bible, New International Version®, NIV®. Copyright © 1973, 1978, 1984, 2011 by Biblica, Inc.TM Used by permission of Zondervan. All rights reserved worldwide. www.zondervan.com. The "NIV" and "New International Version" are trademarks registered in the United States Patent and Trademark Office by Biblica, Inc.TM. Scripture quotations marked ESV are taken from the ESV® Bible (The Holy Bible, English Standard Version®), copyright © 2001 by Crossway Bibles, a publishing ministry of Good News Publishers. Used by permission. All rights reserved.

All rights reserved, including the right to reproduce this book or portions thereof in any form whatsoever.

For information, address Trilogy Christian Publishing

Rights Department, 2442 Michelle Drive, Tustin, Ca 92780.

Trilogy Christian Publishing/ TBN and colophon are trademarks of Trinity Broadcasting Network.

For information about special discounts for bulk purchases, please contact Trilogy Christian Publishing.

Trilogy Disclaimer: The views and content expressed in this book are those of the author and may not necessarily reflect the views and doctrine of Trilogy Christian Publishing or the Trinity Broadcasting Network.

10 9 8 7 6 5 4 3 2 1

Library of Congress Cataloging-in-Publication Data is available.

ISBN 979-8-89333-392-3

ISBN 979-8-89333-393-0 (ebook)

Dedication

For my parents, Richard and Evelyn Pajonas.

Your love is a priceless gift that I carry within my heart. Mere words could never fully describe my infinite love and gratitude for both of you.

For my mother, Carmen Hernandez.
I'll love you always and forever, Mami.

Preface

I was inspired by God to write this book. My journey started when the Holy Spirit delivered one simple sentence to me: "from a caterpillar to a butterfly."

In nature, there is no better representation of transformation than that of a caterpillar becoming a butterfly. It involves true rebirth and a completely new identity, which is exactly what happens to us when we are born again as children of Christ.

Being that my story is one of transformation, I realized what my creator wanted me to do. He wanted me to write my memoir, but it would serve as a vehicle to tell my testimony.

As you read the book, you will notice there are only four chapters, and each refers to a different stage in a caterpillar's life. I also took every stage and related it to what I feel are the corresponding seasons of my life.

My greatest hope lies in what happens once you've finished reading *From Broken to Butterfly*. I pray that after you learn about the miraculous work Jesus has done within me and my life, you will give Him the opportunity to do the same in yours. I also pray that you will come to understand that our best and most beautiful version of self can only be found in Christ. That is our true identity, and I can testify firsthand that it is nothing short of amazing. It's life-changing at its finest because it's in Him that we truly discover who we were created to be.

Nina Pajonas

The Lord bless you and keep you; the Lord make his face shine on you and be gracious to you; the Lord turn his face toward you and give you peace.

Numbers 6:24-26 (NIV)

Acknowledgments

First and foremost, I want to thank God for putting it on my heart to write this book, inspiring the words on the pages, and giving me the faith to complete it.

This book would never have made it from my heart to my publisher without my amazing parents, Richard and Evelyn Pajonas. They continuously expressed their belief in me and what I was doing, which motivated me tremendously throughout my journey. I'm also beyond grateful for their generous financial contribution that helped make my dream become a reality.

My heartfelt "thanks" goes out to my sister, Lisa Pajonas, who provided me with great emotional support as I tackled this deeply personal passion project. Many tears were shed when I revisited past traumas that I was writing about, and Lisa always lent me her steadfast strength during those times.

I'm immensely grateful for my sister, Lisa LeBlanc, who cheered me on ceaselessly while I wrote this book. I'll always treasure the many hours we spent discussing the things that I was learning about myself and God along the way. I also want to thank her husband, Tim LeBlanc, for helping me with the title by delivering a timely spiritual message that I needed to hear.

Saying thank you to my brother, John Melecio, doesn't seem like nearly enough. I will never forget the way he loved and supported me during one of the darkest parts of my story.

I'm eternally grateful that God led me to my church, theCross, in Mount Dora, Florida. The trajectory of my life changed when I walked through their doors in November of 2017 because they helped guide me back to the Lord.

I want to personally thank our lead pastor, Mark Crossman, and executive pastor, Jacob Baumann, for their amazing leadership over the years. I have learned so many valuable spiritual lessons from their sermons and have been blessed to have their pastoral support.

I'm profoundly grateful for Christopher Michael Burns, LCSW, CSAT, my former therapist who became my brother in Christ and mentor. Chris is the Healing Minister at theCross and an incredible man of God. It is clear to me that the Lord utilized Chris as an instrument of change in my life. I can say that with confidence because without Chris's guidance and support, much of Chapter 4 wouldn't have happened.

I want to give special thanks to Linda Crossman, the Women's Ministry director at theCross. She is a wonderful woman of God and a dear friend. Linda has poured into me greatly over the years. Her walk with the Lord inspires me.

I must also thank Kharl Kapp, our Worship Director at theCross. Kharl taught me so much about leading worship, both by example and direction. The years I spent on his team were and always will be special to me.

I'm very grateful for the guidance and encouragement I've received from the Trilogy Christian Publishing team on my journey to becoming a published author. They have blessed me abundantly because they helped me accomplish the assignment God put on my heart.

There aren't enough ways to thank all the people I've met in the twelve-step programs who have helped me on my journey. I've learned so much from all of them. They have taught me how to have an amazing life in recovery.

Finally, I want to express my deepest appreciation and admiration for all the women I've had the honor of meeting over the years who have shared their stories with me. Their vulnerability, resiliency, and strength inspired me more than they could ever know. Without them, I wouldn't have had the courage to tell my story.

Table of Contents

Dedication..4

Preface..5

Acknowledgments..7

Introduction..11

Stage 1—The Expendable Egg...13

Stage 2–The Lonely Larva (Caterpillar)..............................27

Stage 3–The Painful Pupa (Chrysalis).................................63

Stage 4—A Beautiful Butterfly..87

Afterword..154

About the Author...155

Introduction

I was standing in the lobby of a rehab, wondering what had become of me and my life. How did I get here? How did my life come to this?

I watched my father's back as he walked away from me and towards the door. His shoulders were slumped because the weight of my addiction grew too heavy for him to carry. My powerful father, who I cried on as a little girl, was now crying over me. My most valiant protector couldn't slay the dragon of my addiction, and it devastated him.

I almost screamed, "Daddy, don't leave me!" as he opened the door to exit the facility, but somehow I managed not to, though I don't know how. Perhaps it was the last remnants of pride I scraped up from the bottom of my tortured soul. Or maybe it was because I was crying so hysterically that I could barely breathe, let alone speak. Either way, it was just me and my addiction in the lobby after my father left. My addiction had gone everywhere with me for seventeen years. It's impossible to shake your own shadow because it follows you wherever you go.

Finally, in November of 2017, I was trying to break free from my worst enemy. That's why I was standing in the lobby of that rehab.

There was no way I could have known I was on the precipice of a miraculous journey of salvation, redemption, restoration, and transformation. Silly me, I thought I was just there to get sober.

I am eternally grateful that God had even more plans in store for me, but He started that day with my sobriety.

Hi, my name is Nina, and I'm an alcoholic.

That's how I announce myself at every twelve-step meeting I attend. It's how we are all taught to introduce ourselves. We disclose our first names and the addiction we suffer from. It's a frank and vulnerable statement; that's why it's so impactful and meaningful. I go to meetings because they act as medicine for my disease. They help to keep me well both mentally and emotionally. It is very important to understand that there is no cure for addiction and that the best a person can achieve is remission from the disease. I endeavor to stay sober one day at a time, as all people with a substance use disorder do.

I was forty-four years old when I arrived at that rehab. I was finally seeking help for my alcoholism, and the odds were stacked against me. The older someone is, the harder it is for them to succeed in recovery, but thankfully, our Savior doesn't care about statistics. He only cares about salvation. Praise God, I am now fifty years old and have been blessed with over six years of sobriety.

Three crucial factors enabled me to get sober and have helped me remain sober. The first would be my great desire and willingness to change. The second would be my fellowship, where I learn from others who have my disease and support me immensely. The third and most important factor is my relationship with God. Without Him, I wouldn't be alive today.

Make no mistake, my story is about the King of Glory. This book is my testimony; it is an account of what He's done for me and within me.

> *Now to him who is able to do immeasurably more than all we ask or imagine, according to his power that is at work within us, to him be glory in the church and in Christ Jesus throughout all generations, for ever and ever! Amen.*
>
> Ephesians 3:20-21 (NIV)

Stage 1

The Expendable Egg

I was born and raised in Brooklyn, New York. I was the youngest of four children and lived on the second floor of a two-family home with the rest of my family: my father, Richard; my stepmother, Evelyn; my stepsister, Lisa; my stepbrother, John; and my biological sister, Lisa. While on the first floor, my father's brother, George, lived with his wife and their four children. Thirteen of us lived in the house because my grandfather also had an apartment in the basement. It was a very full and hectic house, to say the least.

There were eight kids in total, and it was constant chaos because we were always running upstairs and downstairs to play with one another. After school, you could usually find most of us playing in front of our house or on the block. However, I often chose to stay inside, upstairs by myself, while they all played outside. It was quiet. I could hear myself think. I didn't just like the calm; I needed it.

As God would have it, I discovered my first spiritual gift from Him during one of my "isolation sessions." It happened when I was seven years old while listening to the radio.

Music always had a compelling effect on me as a child. It seemed to demand my attention, and I was a willing captive because I loved to bask in its beauty. Music was my sanctuary. With it, I felt safe to experience all of my emotions. I was very grateful to have a space where I could.

On that particular day, I came home from school and did what I normally did. I waited for my brother and sisters to run downstairs and go outside. As soon as they left, I ran down the stairs, but when I reached the bottom, I locked the door so they couldn't get back in. I would do that same thing time and again. When I heard the lock's bolt sliding into place, it made me giddy! Then I ran back upstairs and sat on the living room floor, right in front of the wood and glass unit that held my parents' stereo system. There was no rhyme or reason as to the music I would listen to on any given day. I would simply turn the silver knob on the stereo back and forth from station to station until I heard something that intrigued me. Sometimes, when I was feeling adventurous, I would go through my parents' vinyl records and play one of them. However, that day the silver knob landed on an opera station, and I heard a soprano hit an incredibly beautiful high note. I was stunned. I kept listening as the music wrapped around me magically. Then, I spontaneously tried to mimic the note the opera singer had sung, and low and behold, it sounded pretty close to my untrained ears! That shocked me, so I tried to do it again and got the same result. Then I wanted to hear what else I could do, so I put on a Barbara Streisand album and started singing along with the vocalist I most admired. I realized I had a lot of work to do, but I knew I had some talent. I was so excited! I was seven years old when I learned that God had blessed me with the gift of singing. That was when I transitioned from being captivated by music to falling in love with it.

I had discovered my passion and purpose. For me, singing was life-affirming. I finally felt I had something of value to offer the world, and I believed that gave me value. Before discovering my talent, I felt weird and out of place, a misfit, but afterward, I felt there was a purpose for my creation and existence in the world. That was an entirely different concept for me because I had never thought so prior. I know that sounds incredibly sad because it is. The spiritual gift that God gave me was not what gave me value. Simply being His child, created in His image, made me priceless to Him, but unfortunately, my seven-year-old mind, heart, and soul could not comprehend such things yet.

After that day, I began to practice my vocals constantly. While my siblings and cousins were outside playing, most of the time, I was inside singing. Although, there were times that I would stop what I was doing to go out on our terrace and watch them play. Watching them made me feel lonely, but that never stopped me from secluding myself. I foolishly thought that the joy I experienced with music would completely fulfill me. I believed that singing would mend my wounded heart. I thought if I sang of my pain and through my pain, I could stop it, but in actuality, I was only projecting it. My musical talent was merely a bandaid and outlet for my insecurities and emotional struggles. Many years would pass before I had the epiphany that as much as I love music, it can't love me back.

Sadly, I hid the thing that gave me so much happiness. I wouldn't practice singing in front of my siblings and refused to tell my parents about my talent. I feared that my joy and newfound identity would be taken from me if I did either. As a child, I was always worried about something or someone. I frequently forecasted doom and gloom in my life, making it difficult to fully experience happiness because I constantly thought about when and how it could end.

Living in fear is such a horror. The irony is that it can make us hold on to something or someone so tightly as not to lose it that we can wind up squeezing the very life out of what we so dearly love.

Unfortunately, I was riddled with anxiety from a very young age because I suffered from abandonment issues. My mother, Carmen, was an alcoholic and medication drug abuser, and her addiction issues were ultimately the reason that my parents got divorced when I was three years old. Initially, my mother got custody, as that was the custom then. However, she had a bad habit of leaving my sister Lisa and me with her parents, and no one knew when she would return. Life was extremely stressful during that time, and even as a child who didn't quite understand what was going on, I felt anger, stress, frustration, fear, and sorrow. Much of it was my own; I realize that now, but I also felt it from the adults around me.

My father, Richard, finally got custody of me and my sister when I was six because my mother relinquished custody of us. By then, he was also remarried to my stepmother Evelyn, and she had two children from her first marriage. She had a daughter named Lisa and a son named John, so I had two older sisters named Lisa! Both my sisters were three years older than me, and my brother John was seven years older than me, so I was the baby of the family.

Once my mother gave up custody of me and my sister, she left again, but this time for a long time. All I would get were postcards in the mail from her saying hi and that she loved me. I remember reading those postcards and thinking, *If you loved me, you would be with me. If you loved me, you never would have left me.* Those were my unspoken thoughts and feelings whenever I got a postcard from her. In a way, I dreaded getting them. I always wanted her to say, "I'll be back home soon. I can't wait to see you!" So when she didn't, it devastated me. I would feel abandoned and unwanted all over again.

I even noticed that the zip codes were changing on her postcards, and I would ask my father why she kept moving and when she was coming back. Of course, he could never give me a straight answer, but he always tried to assure me that she would return. I clung to his assurances just as much as I clung to my father. I was a Daddy's girl, so wherever he was, I wasn't too far behind. I barely let him out of my sight because I was terrified that I'd lose him, too.

The story I told myself about my mother's absence was not that she chose to leave for her misguided reasons but rather that I hadn't been important enough for her to stay. That's why I couldn't understand the purpose of my existence in the world. They say actions speak louder than words, and my mother's actions told me that I was expendable. My broken heart said that she easily discarded me because she didn't love me, and if my mother didn't love me, there must be something wrong with me. I made the blame mine. It was the morbid tale I told myself to understand the behavior of a woman who was in the throes of addiction.

Consequently, that's where my fear of losing people and my happiness began. I thought if my mother could desert me, anyone could, and that they probably would. My immense fear of loss was the result of my mother leaving me and my sister, but then it went on to transfer to my father, my singing, and the future romantic relationships I would have.

That was also when my people-pleasing tendencies began. I desperately wanted the people I loved to be happy with me because I was petrified that they would leave me if they weren't. That wasn't the truth, but that's insignificant. That's what I believed. I developed highly dysfunctional behaviors at a very early age.

I had so many feelings about what had transpired in my life, and I was still very young. I was sad and angry that my life didn't look like everyone else's. It was the 1980s, and divorce was extremely uncommon, so I felt very different from my friends. I essentially had two mothers, but I couldn't tell my friends where my biological one was, and trust me, they asked. I also had two sisters named Lisa, which was comical but confusing and challenging to explain.

First, there was my biological sister, Lisa, who was going through the same experiences I was, feeling forsaken and abandoned. Then, I had a new sister, Lisa, and a new brother named John, who I was getting to know and love. It was a very trying time. We were all just doing our best to put two broken families together and make them whole.

Singing was the glue that held me together. It was my lifeline, my therapy, and my refuge. It was the world I created so that I could escape the world that I was in.

I never spoke about my music to anyone except my sisters, who would mention that they could hear me singing through the door when they came back inside from playing. I would always beg them not to say anything to our parents, and they agreed not to because they knew how shy I was.

Occasionally, my sisters would ask me to sing for them, but I refused to because I didn't want to be critiqued about something I so dearly loved. I didn't want my music to be tainted with outside influences. I always feared that something bad would happen if my two worlds collided.

Finally, after hiding my greatest passion for three years, I realized I no longer wanted to. It had gotten to the point where there was a fire inside of me to create music publicly. I longed to be understood and felt there was no better way to express myself. I wanted to share my soul's song with everyone.

The opportunity came when I was ten, and my parents took us on a family cruise to the Bahamas. While we were on the cruise, they announced that they would have a talent show. As soon as I heard about it, I knew I wanted to audition, but I didn't discuss it with anyone in my family until afterward. I was scared to put myself out there but mustered up all my courage and did it anyway. My favorite song at that time was "You Light Up My Life" by Debbie Boone, so that's what I decided to sing.

On the day of the audition, I walked into the room where they held the shows on the ship. It was an enormous room, and I could see a young man sitting at a piano across it. As I approached him, he looked at me puzzled, as if thinking, *What are you doing here, kid?* However, he said, "Hello, how can I help you?"

I told him I was there because I wanted to sing in the talent show.

The young man replied, "What do you want to sing?"

I smiled brightly and said, "'You Light Up My Life.' I don't know the name of the woman who sings it, but I can sing it like her."

Then he said, "What key do you sing it in?"

I was stumped. I had no clue what he was talking about. I knew nothing about keys, notes, melody, or harmony. I was self-taught; everything I did, I did by ear. So I stood there looking very confused momentarily and then said, "I don't understand what you mean."

I can only imagine that the young man wanted to pull his hair out of his head because he was trying to discuss the intricacies of music with a child, but he was kind enough to say, "Do you sing it lower or higher than she does?"

The song we were discussing is both sad and beautiful. It's about a lonely woman who waits a very long time for her soulmate. Then, she meets him and sings about the light and hope he brings to her life. That's the song I wanted to sing. When I think about it now, the guy probably thought I was crazy.

I replied, "I sing it just like her. Whatever she does, that's how I do it."

Not the best explanation to offer a professional musician, but I think my spunk intrigued him, so he said, "Okay, I'm going to start playing, and I'll tell you when to come in."

So he did. When I started to sing, the young man looked pleasantly surprised, but by the time we got to the second verse, I was stumbling on the words because I didn't know them all.

He stopped playing and said, "Where did you learn to sing like that?" I had no idea what he meant, but he looked pleased, which made me happy. *Maybe I am good enough*, I thought.

Then I wound up telling him my whole story. Everything came rushing out of me in a mixture of excitement and relief. I said, "I sing by myself all the time at home. I sing with the radio, but I don't let anyone hear me because I'm scared they won't like it. I decided to do the talent show because I want to show people what I love to do. Do you think I'm good enough?"

There is no way that young man could have known how much I was asking him with that simple question. "Am I good enough?" was a question I had been asking myself for a very long time, and not just about my singing. His tone was very sweet when he replied that I was a good singer and could be in the talent show. He also said that he would figure out all the words to the song with the band so that I could memorize them. He told me to come by the band's cabin later that evening and that he would give me the words then.

Spontaneously, I hugged him while thanking him profusely for his help. Then I ran out of the room and back to the cabin I was sharing with my sisters. When I got there, I told them everything. They were shocked but thought it was great that I had put myself out there. My sisters hugged me and said they were very proud of me. Then, as older sisters do, they teased me and said, "Does that mean we can hear you sing now?" Afterward, we all started laughing, and then, with a triumphant smile, I shouted, "Yes!"

I'm exceptionally blessed that God gave me two sisters. They both support me incredibly but do so in different ways. However, the result is always the same: after I've been in their presence, I always leave feeling infinitely loved.

Later that night, we sat down for dinner with our parents in the dining hall, and my sisters kept looking at me as if to say, "Tell them already!" I was extremely nervous about telling my parents I had auditioned, especially my father, Richard. I always wanted his approval because I was happy when he was pleased with me, but when he wasn't, I was miserable. That's codependency in a nutshell, and obviously, it's very unhealthy. However, my father never tried to make me feel that way. It was the fear of loss and lack of self-worth I developed after my mother left me that created a dependency on my father that was detrimental to me.

Finally, I worked up the courage to tell him. I said, "Daddy, I'm going to be in the talent show!"

My father looked at me like I said I was going to Mars and said, "What do you mean you're going to be in the talent show? What are you going to do?"

I replied excitedly, "I'm going to sing! I love to sing! I sing all the time at home. I just didn't tell you and Mom about it, but the man from the band said I am good! I have to meet with him and the other band members after dinner so they can give me the words to the song I'm going to sing because I don't know them all."

It all rushed out of me in one long, ecstatic breath. I sat there waiting for him to answer in hopeful anticipation. I thought hearing about my talent would make him proud of me or that he would think I was special. I had a hard time believing that my father loved me for the silly, shy, sensitive, and loving child that I was. I questioned his love because deep down inside, I questioned everyone's love. All because of the lack of love I felt from my mother due to her absence.

Those few moments felt like an eternity, but eventually, he said, "You sing? When did you start singing?" He sounded incredulous and almost annoyed.

One of my sisters piped up and said, "Dad, she's really good. We can hear her singing through the door sometimes, but she made us promise not to tell you. You know how Nina is, she's shy. So, we didn't say anything."

Then, my father said, "Okay, well, take your sisters with you when you get the words from the band, and then come right back." He didn't seem thrilled. Still, he wasn't trying to stop me, so I was satisfied.

Later in life, my father told me he was scared because he didn't know if I could sing. He didn't know if my sisters and the guy from the band were just being nice to me so as not to hurt my feelings. My father said he was worried because I was extremely sensitive, and he could not protect me from a major disappointment if it all didn't go as well as I wanted. My father's sensitive daughter, who hid from the world, was about to put herself on full display. Talk about extremes! I'm sure he was more than scared. He was probably petrified.

The night before the cruise ended, they held the talent show. I was nervous as I sat down at a table with my family in the room where the show was being held. I was the last person to perform.

When they called my name, I walked up to the stage and stood in the spotlight. Everything around me was dark. There were little flickering candles on the tables, with just enough light emanating from them to discern that people were there but not enough to see them clearly. They all looked like shadowy figures that blended into one another. That was perfect because it allowed me to pretend I was singing alone in a big, dark room. I heard the first few notes of the song being played on the piano, and before I knew it, I was singing. Low, husky tones came out of me as I began to sing of loneliness and pain, both of which I knew all too well. Then I sang of the man that would save me from all of it. I hadn't met him at ten years old, but you wouldn't know it from the way my soul sang. It was believable because that's what my heart longed for.

I was halfway through the song when a photographer suddenly emerged in front of me. He had a camera with a massive light on top of it, and as he started taking pictures, giant flashes of light exploded before my face. It felt like they were blinding me. The photographer startled me so much that I stopped singing immediately because I forgot the lyrics. My mind went completely blank.

Time felt like it froze. I could feel everyone's eyes on me when they hadn't been there before. It had just been me and my music in a dark room until that photographer came along.

I have no idea how I managed to compose myself and walk back to the piano, but I did. Once there, I saw the guy from the audition, my newfound friend, who told me I was a good singer. We just looked at each other for what seemed like the longest minute of my young life, and then I said, "Take it from the top, please." A huge smile lit up his face as he nodded in agreement.

When I returned to the front of the stage, he started playing the song from the beginning. Then I began to sing, and amazingly enough, I got lost in the music. My emotions swept me away and into my little world again. Finally, the song ended, and as they say, I left it all on the stage.

Gradually, I became aware of the people around me and realized that the room was silent. You could hear a pin drop. The silence was deafening and made me anxious. I thought to myself, *They didn't like it.*

Then everyone stood up and gave me a standing ovation. I stared at them and wondered why they were all standing, but they were applauding quite loudly. Then it dawned on me; they liked my singing!

Or did they? I started to second-guess myself. Maybe they felt sorry for me because I had forgotten all the words and thought it was sweet that I tried again. So, I ran off the stage and back to my cabin. Once there, I climbed up to the top bunk and started crying. I was so mad at myself! I kept thinking that I should have kept my singing to myself. I wasn't ready. I wasn't good enough.

I heard the cabin door open. It was my parents. I didn't want to look at them because I was embarrassed. I felt utterly humiliated.

Then my father said, "Nina, why did you run off? You were great!"

Still crying, I replied, "You're just saying that because you're my dad. You feel sorry for me, and those people did too!"

Then, he said, "You're wrong. You were wonderful. Why didn't you tell Mommy and me that you could sing?"

I replied, " I was scared to! Singing makes me so happy, and I didn't want anyone to ruin it for me."

I finally told my father the truth. After I said that, he looked sad but then went on to say, "You're a good singer, and we are very proud of you for starting again when you forgot the words. You need someone to teach you so you can keep getting better. Do you want us to get you vocal lessons when we get back home?"

Immediately and excitedly, I replied, "Yes!"

Anxiety weighs down the heart, but a kind word cheers it up.

Proverbs 12:25

I finally realized that hiding my music from my parents had limited my joy. I hadn't trusted them with my dream, which kept me from making it a reality. I wanted to be a professional singer, and after hearing everything my father said that night, I thought it was possible! My father's belief in me and my singing made me feel invincible.

Soon after returning from the cruise, I started taking vocal lessons. I also started singing in school and began trying out for leads in the choir.

However, as happy as I was to live in the light with my music, I still missed my mother immensely. In a way, it made her absence even more pronounced because my mother, the woman who gave me life, had no idea what was going on in mine.

About six months later, my mother, Carmen, returned. Praise God that when she did, she was sober.

I was ecstatic when my mother returned because I finally felt I had someone I could identify with, both physically and emotionally. It was uncanny how much I looked like her; people would remark on it wherever we went. My personality was also like hers. We were both highly sensitive and emotional and wore our hearts on our sleeves. I felt at home with my mother because I related to her in almost every way.

When I told my mother about my singing, she was thrilled and told everyone she knew about it. Of course, I would get embarrassed when she did that, but deep down inside, I loved it. She was so proud of me, and through words and actions, she never stopped telling me that. However, the most important thing to me was that my mother, Carmen, loved the essence of me, my heart and soul. I had a beautiful relationship with my mother in which I felt cherished, loved, and infinitely special.

It's heartbreaking to admit that I still struggled with fear of loss and lack of self-worth even after my mother came back. You would think that the emotional chasm she created by her absence would have been filled by her presence, but it wasn't. I still didn't comprehend how she could have ever left in the first place, so my heart remained confused and insecure. I wish that my father's steadfast love could have made everything better, but trauma is tricky, and healing from it doesn't work that way. It's just not that straightforward.

My father's love was and still is like the vast, deep, seemingly endless ocean. To this day, he is still my protector, champion, and best friend. My stepmother Evelyn also loves me tremendously and wonderfully. She is quite possibly the most maternal woman I know. When Evelyn first met me, she immediately took me under her wing because she saw a scared, hurt, and confused child. She knew I needed a mother and immediately filled the vacancy. My stepmother loved and cared for me as if I were her own, and she still does. I was incredibly blessed to have had both parents after my mother's departure. However, a child's heart is delicate, and mine was never quite the same. The wound created by my mother never fully healed. I always felt expendable.

Stage 2

The Lonely Larva (Caterpillar)

Fear of loss plagued me. It started in my childhood, as I discussed, but I would continue to carry that burden into my teenage years, young adulthood, and beyond. It influenced so many decisions that I made. Even worse, the older I got, the greater my fear became. So, it was inevitable that it would go on to affect my romantic relationships. No one makes wise choices based on fear, and my love life perfectly illustrated that.

Oddly enough, I was always drawn to relationships that I knew ultimately would not work out. Unfortunately, it didn't even matter to me if the men were honest about their limitations. It only made me more determined to change their minds. I was convinced that if I got them to commit to me it would prove that I had worth. Such warped thinking, I know, but I'm being completely honest. It was self-sabotaging behavior at its finest, which led to a self-fulfilled prophecy.

I finally came to understand why I did this after an intense examination of my fears. I realized that I entered into relationships that had no hope of survival for two reasons: the first being that I honestly didn't think anyone would love me enough to make me their wife, and the second was that I feared they would ultimately leave me if they ever did.

Three romantic relationships in my life would destroy me in different ways. Each would break my heart horribly for various reasons.

My first love would teach me the harsh lesson of betrayal and that love does not conquer all. My second would make me a mother, briefly, which would serve as a catalyst for my alcoholism. While the third, my last relationship to date, would almost cost me my life.

I will begin when I fell in love for the first time when I was fifteen. It was love at first sight. I was auditioning for the play *Grease* and singing on stage, trying out for the part of Sandy, when I saw him.

He was so handsome. I didn't know his name and had never laid eyes on him before, but that didn't stop my heart from beating wildly at the sight of him. That confused me because I never had a physical reaction like that to someone before. I tried to concentrate on my singing, but it was difficult because he kept staring at me and smiling.

When I finally got off the stage, I returned to the audience and sat in the row in front of him. I could still feel his eyes on me, and I was nervous because I had no idea what to do. Then I felt someone tap me on my shoulder; it was my friend Kelly. I could only focus on the mystery man the entire time I was singing on stage, so I hadn't noticed her sitting beside him. Kelly complimented me on my singing and introduced me to her friend. His name was Ryan.

I was face to face with him, and my heart started its erratic dance again. He said I sang beautifully and asked why he had never met me, almost like he wanted to know where I had been hiding. I felt like asking him the same question but didn't. It seemed like he appeared out of thin air, my Prince Charming. I had read all the fairytales as a little girl who told me he would come for me one day, and there he was. Or so my heart thought. He left soon afterward, and I immediately felt bereft. However, after he was gone, my friend Kelly told me he liked me and asked if she could give him my phone number. Of course, I said, "Yes."

So began my romance with Ryan. He was handsome and charming. He had a chiseled jaw, full lips, and hazel eyes that changed colors on a whim, much like his commitment to me.

Ryan could never make up his mind when it came to our relationship. Either he liked me and wanted to be with me, or he was distant and wanted to see other people. Back and forth we would go. Unfortunately, I was naive and loyal to a fault, which is a very dangerous combination for the heart. It was quite easy for him to manipulate me. My loyalty was one of my biggest flaws because I gave it to the wrong people, men in particular, but it started with Ryan. He was everything to me, and I wanted no one else. I even tried to date during some of our "breaks," if only to show him I could also move on. However, all that did was make Ryan jealous enough to return to me briefly to reestablish his stronghold on my life. Then, he would leave me again when he felt all was secure. Once Ryan got me away from the competition, he was satisfied. Afterward, I would go back to being single and waiting on him, and Ryan would go back to playing the field.

Unfortunately, that destructive dynamic went on for two years. Despite the heartache and disappointment, I remained committed. Sadly, it was during this time that I developed self-destructive patterns of behavior that I would bring into my future relationships.

The first was making allowances for a man who didn't value or cherish me the way he should. The second was convincing myself of a reality I wanted to see rather than acknowledging the truth of what it was.

It was in this toxic relationship that I first learned how to lie to myself. I believed that I would be his wife one day. That was my dream and expectation. I was convinced that the other women were merely distractions, nothing more. I thought it significant that he always came back to me. I thought the fact that he didn't want me to be with other men meant that he ultimately wanted to be with me.

I refused to see his manipulation for what it was: self-centered and cruel, with a complete disregard for my emotional wants and needs.

There seemed to be two rules in our relationship. The first was that Ryan would be my one and only, and the second was that I would be one of many. He took me for granted, and I constantly fueled his ego with my unconditional love and devotion. My loyalty was used against me as a weapon, and Ryan was very effective at wounding me deeply with it. He used to call me his "good girl," which was my title for remaining loyal and faithful to a man who couldn't be either.

Finally, when I was seventeen, we were on our longest stretch of exclusivity. Ryan seemed ready to commit and was making it clear to everyone that we were together. I was so happy. I told myself that all the waiting and heartache had been worth it. I was finally his one and only, or so I thought.

I'll never forget the day when I found out from my cousin, Tim, that Ryan was cheating on me. He said he saw Ryan and a girl walking hand in hand. It will sound strange, but what cut me the deepest was when Tim specified that Ryan was holding her hand. I asked Tim if he was sure, and he said he was because that's how he knew they weren't just friends. Then, Tim said something that struck me deeply: "Friends don't hold hands, cuz."

My heart broke because it was always such a battle to get Ryan to hold my hand, and I never understood why. I started crying, and my mind was racing because it was trying to figure out what my heart couldn't. I wanted to understand what was wrong with me. I mean, it had to be me, right? It had to be my fault. I must be lacking certain things if Ryan didn't love me the way I wanted him to. Maybe it was my looks or personality. Perhaps I wasn't pretty enough or exciting enough for him.

That was when I invented another horrible story about myself to explain the hurtful actions of another. I made the fault mine when it wasn't. It was his. Ryan lacked commitment, loyalty, and honesty.

He lacked integrity and sincerity. However, instead of realizing those things and accepting those truths, I blamed myself. I declared myself unlovable because Ryan didn't love me.

What broke my heart the most was not that Ryan didn't want to hold my hand; it was what it signified. That was his silent declaration that he had no desire to hold onto me. That's what Ryan had been saying with all of his actions over the years. I just failed to believe or accept it. They say that love is blind, and it really can be when it's something we don't want to see. We can tie a blindfold over our own eyes when our reality doesn't measure up to our fantasy.

I was in shock, even though I shouldn't have been. What did I expect after all the inconsistency and waiting? Ryan had dangled the promise of an exclusive relationship over my head for years. Just when I thought I grasped it, he would yank it away from me. He had done that over and over again during our relationship. It was such a tiring, frustrating, painful, and sad dance, yet I never changed partners.

My foolish heart had expected love, commitment, appreciation, and marriage when we were older. Accepting the reality of the situation instead of my version of it was a very rude awakening from my delusional dream.

After waiting two years for him to love me, I finally broke up with Ryan.

Sadly, I didn't know another type of heartbreak would befall me. A few weeks later, in December, my mother Carmen died.

I saw her the day before she died, and before I left, we had a very emotional conversation. During it, she asked me to promise her something, which alarmed me because she had never done that before. My mother, Carmen, made me promise that I would continue to sing. She said, "Nini, your voice is a gift from God; it's special, and you need to share it with the world." I assured her I would, and she persisted, saying, "Promise me."

So I did. I thought it would be an easy promise to keep because I was incredibly passionate about singing then. Unfortunately, I didn't realize what the future would hold for me. I had no clue that I would become an alcoholic ten years later, suffering from the same addiction that my mother had. I had no idea that was coming, so I made her a promise that would haunt me for almost thirty years.

As I left my mother's home that day, I knew it would be the last time I saw her. She left me with that promise and so many beautiful declarations of her love. I had a connection with my mother that I can't explain, and my last conversation with her told my heart that our story was coming to an end. Intuitively, I knew she was saying goodbye.

However, that didn't prevent me from being completely devastated the next day when I got the phone call that she had passed.

My mother had gotten diagnosed with breast cancer not too long after she returned to me and my sister. It was terrible. First, her addiction took her away from us, and then there was the ever-looming threat of breast cancer that she battled for years. I was always terrified of losing her again because it seemed to me that she was only on loan to me from the Lord. My mother had endured a double mastectomy, radiation, and chemotherapy over the years. The doctors initially gave her a year to live and told her to write her will, but my mother dismissed what they said. She told me she prayed to the Lord, asking Him to let her live long enough to see my sister and me graduate high school. I'm happy to say that the Lord was generous because He gave her exactly what she asked for. My mother did get to see us graduate high school before she died because my sister and I both skipped a grade and graduated early.

I know with all my heart and soul that my mother's faith kept her alive for all those years after her initial diagnosis. Faith is so powerful; her faith in the Lord gave us far more years together than we would have had. Of that, I am certain.

Despite all she had been through, no one could have seen her death coming. My mother was in remission from breast cancer at the time, and all seemed to be well. So, when I received the call that my mother had died of cardiac arrest, it felt like life had played a very cruel trick on me. I was gutted because my greatest fears of losing her and my joy had come to fruition.

After my mother's death, a friend of mine asked if she could call Ryan to let him know. Initially, I told her no, but she convinced me that it was the right thing to do, saying he would want to pay his respects. So I agreed to let her tell him. Soon afterward, I saw Ryan, and he told me that he had ended things with the other girl. He apologized profusely and said he wanted us to be together again. I wish I had told him no, but I didn't. Instead, in my overwhelming grief, I decided to give our relationship another chance.

Ryan never met my mother, Carmen, during our two years together. I wanted him to, but he would always cancel the plans I made for them to meet. Eventually, my mother told me not to try anymore. When I think about it now, she knew what I didn't want to know; he had no desire to meet her.

The first time Ryan ever laid eyes on my mother, he was at her wake, and she was in a coffin.

My mother's wake was packed with people. A line outside the funeral home stretched down the block and around the corner with people waiting to come in to pay their respects. It touched my heart immensely because while my mother might not have had much money, she was rich in love and faith. Her life was rooted in intangible things of the greatest value, and the people there represented how that impacted their lives. It was beautiful to witness the lives my mother Carmen had touched and to hear their stories and remembrances of her.

I was always proud to be my mother's daughter because I admired how she loved others. She loved completely and without reservation, holding nothing back. She never judged others, though she was her own worst critique. My mother's capacity and ability to love others seemed limitless, yet I know she sometimes struggled to love herself.

I tried my best to be the dutiful daughter. I walked around greeting everyone and thanked them for being there. I could hear the whispered comments of people talking to one another, saying, "She is the spitting image of her mother" and "It's like looking at Carmen!" For some, I think the striking resemblance I had to my mother made them uneasy, while for others, I believe it offered some small measure of comfort.

As for me, I was crawling out of my skin. Being an introvert, I was severely anxious about being surrounded by so many people; all I wanted to do was crawl up into the fetal position and cry. I thought I would scream if I heard "I'm so sorry…" one more time. I couldn't believe people dared say, "Well, she was sick for a very long time." I was mentally and emotionally exhausted. The small talk and platitudes grew tiresome and aggravating very quickly. What I wanted to do was scream at the top of my lungs to the crowded room, saying, "My mother was in remission from cancer! She was finally supposed to be okay! I didn't have enough time with her! I'm only seventeen years old; I shouldn't be burying my mother!"

Inside, it felt like pieces of me were breaking apart bit by bit while despair was settling into my soul. Despite my emotional agony, I smiled tactfully and said, "Thank you for coming," while shaking their hands and moving on to the next person.

During my mother's wake, I started to develop my polished persona. It was the facade I learned to erect at a moment's notice to convince people that I was well when I wasn't. I would pretend that I had it all together when, in reality, I was falling apart right in front of their eyes.

About halfway through the wake, I saw that Ryan had entered the room. I felt his presence before I even saw him. As soon as we locked eyes, he started to walk toward me. I could feel my vulnerability and sorrow rising to the surface, but when he took me into his arms, I finally felt safe.

In all the time I had been with Ryan, I never felt like I could lean on him, but that night, it was different. He had finally shown up for me and was the man I needed him to be. He asked me to come with him to my mother's casket, and when he looked down at her, he said to me, "She's beautiful. That's where you get it from." Oddly, that was the first and only time Ryan ever called me beautiful. Then he reached out to touch my mother's hand and spoke to her, saying that he wished they had met while she was alive. Ryan also told her that he would look after me. He prayed over her and told her to rest in peace. Then Ryan looked at me and asked if I wanted to say anything to my mother. I told him that I had already spoken to her before everyone came. What happened next shocked me. Ryan asked me if I had touched her, and I said no. I couldn't bring myself to, and I told him so, but he insisted that I should. He said, "It will be the last time you ever see or touch your mother." So he took my hand in his and put our hands on her hand. We stood there for a few minutes, and he said, "Tell her that you love her, say goodbye to your mother, Nina."

I started to cry profusely. I told her that I loved her with all my heart and soul. I told her how much I missed her already. I told her that she was an amazing mother and my best friend. I finally opened up my heart and let the pain pour out.

Ryan supported me in my grief in a way I never could have imagined. That night, during those moments, he was the man I always thought he was and wanted him to be. However, it would prove to be unfortunate for me that my undying devotion to Ryan was reignited that night, along with my love.

About a month after my mother's death, Ryan moved to Georgia. Before our break up, his mother had decided that they would move that January, and we agreed to have a long-distance relationship until

I was old enough to move out of my parents' house. When we got back together, we had fully recommitted ourselves to that plan.

Ryan and I were writing and calling each other constantly, and it seemed as though everything we had been through brought us even closer together. Ryan had reclaimed my love and loyalty because of the way he cared for me after my mother's death. Despite our destructive past and the physical distance between us, I started to believe again that it would all work out.

Unfortunately, the tragedy in my life would continue. Only a few months after my mother's death, I was raped. I'll call him Lucifer because he might as well have been the devil incarnate.

Lucifer was someone I met through mutual friends. We weren't close by any stretch of the imagination, but we ran into each other often enough for me to realize that he was attracted to me.

In fact, only a few weeks before he raped me, he had asked me out. At the time, I quickly but kindly told him no and explained that I had a boyfriend. However, that didn't stop him in the slightest. I was shocked when Lucifer said that he heard my boyfriend didn't live in New York anymore and that long-distance relationships were a joke. In retrospect, it should have also scared me because he obviously had no respect for my relationship or me. I had already told him I wasn't interested and that I was committed to someone else, yet he still persisted.

One of the things that haunts me the most about the day I was raped was that it could have been avoided. If I had trusted my gut and followed my parent's rules, it never would have happened.

I had come home after school and was getting ready to start my homework when my phone rang; it was Lucifer. Angrily, I asked him how he got my phone number, and he said that one of my friends gave it to him. He asked me not to get mad at them and then went on to say why he was calling. Lucifer told me his best friend's mother died and said that she was like a mother to him. He said he was devastated. Then he said, "I heard your mom just died, so I knew you would understand what I'm going through."

To this day, it infuriates me that he used my mother's death as emotional bait, but I guess nothing is off-limits to a rapist.

As soon as he mentioned my mother's death, I felt my heart soften. I also felt guilty for being angry about his call initially. Then, like a predator sensing his prey was ready for the kill, he asked me if I would meet him at his apartment so we could talk. He also said he wanted me to help him pick out clothes for the funeral because he had never gone to one before. The lies came out of his mouth easily and convincingly. Lucifer was also quick to say that other people would be there, adults specifically.

At first, I objected. My parents had never met him and that was a rule in our house; we weren't allowed to go out with anyone unless our parents had met them. I didn't like the guy, and everything inside me told me that it was a bad idea, but even in my grief, I had a compassionate heart. So, I went.

I left my house and drove over to his apartment complex. I had never driven to that area before, and this way before GPS, so it took me a while to get there, long enough for me to keep questioning my decision to go. I felt guilty about breaking my parent's rules but justified my decision by focusing on the fact that I was trying to help someone in need.

When I finally got there, I found the building he lived in and went inside. I walked down the hallway very slowly, all the while looking at the numbers on the doors so I could find the right one. However, I felt extremely conflicted. I was still debating whether I should go back home, but I thought that would be a cruel and heartless thing to do, so I continued walking until I was in front of his door.

When he opened it, he thanked me for coming, and I walked inside. As soon as I did, he closed the door and locked it behind me. Immediately, I looked around and saw that no one was there. Fear and regret had my heart beating erratically, but it was too late. I wasn't in his home for more than a couple of minutes before he attacked me.

I tried my best to fight him off. I even managed to push him off of me three times, much to his surprise, but it wasn't enough. Lucifer was too quick and too strong, so he didn't stay down for long. The fourth time he attacked me, I wasn't able to fight him off, and he raped me.

I have only had one out-of-body experience in my life, and it happened on that day. As he violated me physically, I detached psychologically. I was no longer there. Instead, I seemed to be watching everything happen from up above, as if I were floating and hovering over the evil situation that was unfolding.

Afterward, Lucifer got up like nothing happened. He just walked into his bathroom and started shaving. He didn't have a care in the world.

It took me several minutes to get myself together, but once I did, I walked over to the bathroom and stood behind him. I wasn't scared of him anymore because, in my mind, he'd already done his worst to me. As I stood behind him, I stared at his reflection in the mirror with a look of utter hatred on my face.

Then, he smiled at me.

When I saw him smile, I wanted to do the unthinkable, but stopped myself. I felt myself shaking with fury. My flesh demanded that he be destroyed because he destroyed me, but then I saw my face in the mirror again. A wild-eyed, crazy woman was looking back at me, and I didn't recognize her. That was when the Lord told me to stop. I became even more furious when I received that command! I wanted vengeance to be mine! I wanted him to suffer, but the Lord said no. He didn't want me to become the darkness. He didn't want the enemy to win.

> *Be alert and of sober mind. Your enemy the devil prowls around like a roaring lion looking for someone to devour.*
>
> 1 Peter 5:8 (NIV)

Obedience at a time like that is beyond difficult, but thankfully, I did listen to the Lord.

As I walked out of the bathroom and his apartment, I was eerily calm. I can only imagine that I looked like a zombie because I felt like the living dead. I didn't even cry when I finally got to my car. I just put my key in the ignition and drove away. I functioned on autopilot the entire drive home.

When I walked into my house and saw my family I made up a lie about where I'd been and what I'd been doing. Then I told everyone that I didn't feel well so that they would leave me alone.

In the weeks that followed, I started acting out a lot, which wasn't like me at all. Finally, one night, after I had broken curfew once again, my stepmother Evelyn sat me down. She wanted to know why I wasn't following the rules of the house. She told me that I wasn't behaving normally and that she was worried about me. Hearing the concern in her voice was what brought me to tears, finally. I hadn't cried since being raped, and then it felt like I couldn't stop.

Immediately, my stepmother Evelyn went to get my father, and I told him everything. I can't even begin to describe how exceedingly painful that was. Seeing the look of devastation on my father's face annihilated me emotionally. I'd never seen that look before, and it made me grieve for him too.

My family wanted me to press charges, but I refused. My father, Richard, was a police officer, so I knew how most rape cases were handled. It's unfortunate, but back then, the victim was treated horribly. They were raked over the coals within the court system, left to defend themselves against a series of legal attacks to prove their innocence in the matter. I told my father I didn't have it in me to endure that after everything I'd been through, and he understood. So, instead, we opted for counseling. That was the first time in my life that I would go to see a therapist, but it wouldn't be the last.

The rape was a defining moment in my life because it ultimately destroyed my faith. I could not understand why God would allow that to happen to me, especially right after losing my mother. I felt forsaken. I realize now that I thought that God had abandoned me, just like my mother had when I was a young child. In my juvenile spiritual condition, I blamed God for breaking what was left of my heart.

The pain was unbearable, so I turned to Ryan and told him about the rape. That was a very difficult decision for me to make because the rape left me feeling emotionally raw and highly fragile. That type of vulnerability is excruciating after such a trauma. The wound is so incredibly deep, and it is infected with shame, even though it's not yours to own.

I felt like I might never get Lucifer's stain off my soul. I also worried that Ryan wouldn't think of me as his "good girl" anymore, although he assured me that wasn't the case. I felt dead inside, and I wanted Ryan to love me back to life. He told me to come to Georgia to visit him so that we could spend time together and he could help me heal. That was the plan anyway, but Ryan's track record spoke more of his capacity to disappoint than his ability to be dependable, so I guess it was inevitable that he would return to his old ways.

I saved up my money and flew out to Georgia. My biological sister Lisa lived there then and picked me up from the airport. Immediately, we went to a payphone, and I called Ryan. When he picked up, Ryan told me he couldn't see me because he couldn't get time off from work. By the time I got to Georgia, it was almost two months after the rape, so there had been plenty of time for him to arrange things with his job. After he said that to me, I cursed at him, which I had never done before, and hung up the phone by slamming it down. Then I picked up the phone and started smashing it against the phone booth. I went crazy. My sister had to stop me and drag me back into her car.

Ryan's actions convinced me he thought I wasn't a "good girl" anymore. No matter how hard anyone tried, they could not convince me that Ryan wasn't disgusted by what happened to me. As a result, I carried those horrible thoughts and feelings around with me for a very long time. Far longer than I care to admit. It was very difficult for my mind, heart, and soul to accept that he could be so cruel and desert me when I needed him the most, but unfortunately, that's precisely what he did.

I seriously started to question my self-worth after Ryan abandoned me during what was the most condensed year of trauma in my life. I was in shambles emotionally, and he made it very clear that he didn't want to be there to deal with it or me. I even reached out to him when I got home to see if he would apologize, but he never responded.

Left with what seemed like a million questions and an utterly devastated and broken heart, I came up with my own answers. The destructive, dysfunctional, and desperate answers of a young girl who couldn't make sense of all the pain she was enduring. I ultimately decided that his actions and decisions were further proof that the love I offered to others was worthless. I concluded there was nothing special about me because he could leave me easily without any explanation. He just disappeared, much like my mother did when I was a child. Although I could not make the correlation then, I do now. The wound my mother inflicted never really healed, so his behavior just widened an already gaping wound and infected it.

I couldn't eat and started losing weight. I also suffered from insomnia for quite a while. My moods were volatile. I would bounce back and forth with a myriad of emotions. I was bitter, angry, disgusted, fearful, depressed, and anxious. Cynicism also reared its ugly head, and I started questioning everything about people and life. I was grieving after severe trauma and an enormous betrayal. I was mourning my mother's death, the death of my innocence, and the death of my relationship with my first love. It seemed that death was all around me, so it didn't take long before it made its way inside.

> *Godly sorrow brings repentance that leads to salvation and leaves no regret, but worldly sorrow brings death.*
>
> 2 Corinthians 7:10 (NIV)

I couldn't find my faith; it was as if it had disappeared. I couldn't feel God near me like I normally did, but I didn't attribute it to the fact that I had pushed Him away during my sorrow.

Through it all, the worst part was that I didn't have my mother to turn to. My beautiful mother, whose faith inspired mine and who had taught me everything I knew about God.

When I was a child, my mother would tuck me into bed at night and guide me in praying to the Lord. Afterward, she would give me "butterfly kisses," which was what she called it when she put her eyelashes on my cheeks and fluttered them. I have so many wonderful memories of her, and many of them are centered around God. She had the most exquisite, resolute, pure faith I have ever witnessed.

My mother understood me best, probably because I was so much like her. No one has ever quite comprehended my soul like my mother Carmen did. I needed her more than ever, and she was gone.

The loss of a parent is an agonizing pain that I wish no one had to endure, but sadly, the cycle of life doesn't allow for that. I had an extraordinary connection with my mother, Carmen. My mother represented the missing pieces to the puzzle that was me; with her passing, they were gone forever.

It felt like my heart and soul had been shattered into a thousand pieces. I might not have felt whole after my mother's death, but after the rape, I didn't even feel human. I wasn't just uncomfortable in my skin; I hated my skin. I wanted to be anyone else but me because the pain was devastating.

I had suffered condensed and severe trauma, and as hard as I tried to move forward, I just couldn't, at least not in a healthy way. Unfortunately, I was never the same afterward. It didn't happen overnight, but eventually, those tragedies began to define me, and sorrow became my identity. I believed that my life would be a series of tragic events. I constantly braced myself for more pain and trauma. I didn't just fear that bad things would happen to me; I expected them to. By succumbing to sorrow, I had allowed it to saturate my soul.

Everything transpired during my first semester of college, and while I tried my best to concentrate on my studies, I just couldn't. My studies seemed trivial in comparison to the turmoil that was my life. I also felt that I had nothing in common with the other students. I watched them from afar with their seemingly blissful and carefree lives and felt like an alien from another planet. I couldn't relate to them at all. Eventually, I left college, much to my father's disappointment.

All the trauma I endured caused me to shrink into myself again like I had as a child. I didn't have the emotional tools to triumph over tragedy, and I wouldn't for many years.

Soon after leaving college, I worked a couple of clerical jobs, but they weren't for me. Eventually, I discovered sales. Sales suited me perfectly because it encouraged me to utilize the dysfunctional skills I developed as a byproduct of my people-pleasing personality and co-dependent nature.

I always tried to control how people felt about me because I wanted their approval. When they liked me, I liked me. Otherwise, I felt very insecure and uncomfortable.

In sales, I used my hyper-vigilant nature to analyze every nuance of someone's demeanor to discern who I needed to be and what I needed to do to get them to buy. For me, being a salesperson was just an extension of the life I was already living because it was effortless for me to become what someone else wanted me to be.

I'm very sad to say that being myself was what I found difficult. I didn't see my value at all, so it makes sense that I struggled greatly to like and love myself. I was never comfortable in my skin, so it felt necessary and natural to create the skin of another.

My twenties consisted of mainly three things: working on my sales career, wasting most of the decade in another broken relationship, and hanging out in bars. The only area of productivity was my career, where I made some tremendous strides. However, my love life and social life were very detrimental to me. I wasn't merely treading water in those areas; I was drifting further and further out to sea, and my soul was growing weary. Spiritually, I was very ill, but I didn't recognize it because I was still quite distanced from God.

In my early twenties, I fell in love for the second time with a man named Sal. I didn't see it coming because it started as a friendship.

Sal had a larger-than-life personality. He was unconventionally handsome, charming, and hilarious. He had charisma oozing from every pore. It was almost impossible to dislike Sal. He had the rare ability to disarm people quickly and make them feel like they knew him forever. I love a man who can make me laugh, and Sal made me laugh often, at myself, at him, and good-naturedly at life. The world seemed safer to me with him because he was a man's man, and even as my friend, he was very protective of me. Life had color again with him in it. He was a breath of fresh air after the stench of death and devastation that had permeated my life only a handful of years earlier. Sal felt like a balm for my wounded heart because he restored my hope in people, life, and love. Although I know now that is a responsibility that no person should carry. It wasn't fair to Sal that

I looked to him for those things, and it wasn't healthy for me. It was very foolish of me to allow anyone to wield that kind of power over my emotions, but I didn't realize what I was doing at the time.

At first, we were just friends. Sal even used to call me "kid" because I was younger than him, but that didn't last long because we both started to develop feelings for one another. The only problem with that was that Sal was already in a relationship. He wasn't married, but that doesn't matter. It was still very hurtful and inappropriate behavior. I validated my actions by reflecting on the girl who went after Ryan while I was going out with him, the one he cheated on me with. Years later, I heard they even got married. I convinced myself that I didn't have to care about Sal's girlfriend's feelings because another woman hadn't cared about mine.

Resentment kills a fool, and envy slays the simple.

Job 5:2 (NIV)

I'm not proud of my decisions within this relationship, but in retrospect, I realize that I was looking at life through eyes of bitterness and resentment. They say that eyes are the windows to the soul, which can be interpreted as the state of our souls dictating how we see things. That is the filter through which all experiences get processed. If my spiritual state is weak, the condition of my soul unhealthy, then it can't filter things with faith. Instead, it gets sullied with worldly thinking, leading to worldly behaviors.

That was what happened to me as a result of my pain and trauma and my decision to walk away from God because of it. My soul was slowly but surely compromised, and I was operating from a destructive and sinful space.

> *The eye is the lamp of the body. If your eyes are healthy, your whole body will be full of light. But if your eyes are unhealthy, your whole body will be full of darkness. If then the light within you is darkness, how great is that darkness!*
>
> Matthew 6:22–23 (NIV)

My relationship with Sal lasted five years, during which we were on and off. I was in yet another dysfunctional relationship where I was not prioritized. I accepted the role of the other woman, so there was no need for him to choose or make a commitment. Instead, Sal had us both. She unwittingly and me willingly. It's not that I didn't try to end it or put my foot down, so to speak, but he didn't take me seriously because I wasn't strong enough to demand more from the very beginning.

I always tried to downplay what I was doing by telling myself, "It's not like he's married," which was my mindset when I went to Sal's house one night to see him. It was not a surprise visit; we had plans, and his behavior wasn't unusual in any way. That makes what happened next even more bizarre because I had no reason to be suspicious.

I was sitting at Sal's dining room table when he left the room to go to the bathroom. As I sat there, I looked at the table littered with mail and random pieces of paper, and then I saw a piece of paper that was folded up. There might as well have been a spotlight on it with the way I kept staring at it, and I felt compelled to pick it up. That was strange because I had never snooped through Sal's things prior, but that folded piece of paper seemed to beckon me.

So, I picked it up and started reading, "Dear Sal, I can't believe we're engaged! I'm so happy…" That's as far as I got. I folded the paper and put it back where I found it. Then I waited, seething with anger at Sal and myself. When he came out of the bathroom, he took one look at me and knew something was wrong. I asked him if there was anything he wanted to tell me, and Sal said no. So I reached for the paper and picked it up again.

After I did, his eyes looked like they would fall out of his head. He stood there in shock because he knew exactly what it was. Oddly enough, the first thing Sal said wasn't "sorry," but rather, "Out of all the papers on that table, what in the world made you pick that one up? That particular one! Are you kidding me?" Of course, I told him that didn't matter and screamed at him for not telling me about their engagement. It was a very ugly night, and it finally forced me to end things with Sal.

Afterward, I was depressed that I had wasted even more time in another dead-end relationship and that I had compromised my morals. So, to feel better about myself, I put myself on a diet and started working out to lose weight.

I started my journey of self-improvement with the physical, which was a huge mistake. It was my spiritual and emotional state that needed tending to. I embarked on a transformation of the surface when I needed one of the soul. It was regrettable for me and those who loved me that my grievous error in judgment wound up being my demise.

A few months after ending things with Sal, he called me. He asked if he could see me, saying he felt horrible about what happened. Logically, I knew it wasn't a good idea because Sal made me feel like there was no one else in the world but us. Over the years, that feeling allowed me to get lost in the moments we shared instead of focusing on the reality of the situation. The feelings of shame and self-deprecation would always come afterward on my drive home or the next day when the heady feeling dissipated. However, against my better judgment, I agreed to meet him.

I made that decision because deep down inside, I hoped Sal would tell me that he had changed his mind. I'm embarrassed to say the other reason because it's so shallow, but I wanted him to see all the weight I lost. I wanted Sal to regret his decision and reconsider his choice when he saw me.

> *Pride goes before destruction, a haughty spirit before a fall.*
>
> Proverbs 16:18 (NIV)

When I saw Sal, he reacted to my weight loss but didn't change his mind. He was apologetic and remorseful that he had hurt me, but he still didn't choose me.

Then we started reminiscing, eventually leading us to do something we would soon regret. We were intimate, but we both felt very conflicted about it afterward. When we parted ways, I told Sal that I thought it best that we have no further contact whatsoever. He balked at the idea, saying we could still be friends if we didn't see one another, but I disagreed. I knew I couldn't move on if I were still speaking to him, so Sal finally agreed to respect my decision.

However, I would be the one to break the silence when I called Sal over a month later to tell him that I was pregnant. When I told him, Sal was stunned and asked me what I wanted to do.

I wish wholeheartedly that I hadn't even considered it a decision but rather a certainty that I would have our baby, but I didn't. My biggest concern was what my father would think of me. Not my heavenly father, my biological one.

My father was extremely old-fashioned, and we were raised not to have a child out of wedlock. I thought he would be disgusted with me and convinced myself that he would disown me. All of which was completely untrue, but I was wracked with guilt that I would disgrace our family in such a way. I wasn't going to marry Sal, and he was planning to marry someone else, so I told Sal that I would get an abortion.

My people-pleasing and co-dependent personality cost me the life of my unborn child. My immense fear of abandonment dictated a decision that has weighed heavily on my soul to this day.

At that point and time, I was hanging on by a thread, but it was not the thread of His garment. Had my faith been full and vibrant, I would have made a different choice. I would have chosen to be a mother, and I would be one today. I wish my relationship with the Lord had been filled with faith, hope, and love because that decision was ultimately the death of me spiritually. My shame severed any remaining ties I had with our Lord and Savior, not because He cut the ties that bound us, but because I did.

If anyone were to ask me what day in my life I wish I could live again so that I could live it differently, it would be the day I got the abortion. Not the day I got raped, not the day my mother died, and not the day I almost died, which I will discuss later. If I could go back in time and change one thing, I would choose life for my baby instead of death.

I tried to console myself with the thought that I would be a mother later in life, that I would inevitably get pregnant again and have a child or two. Little did I know that I would never get pregnant again and that the death of my child was also the death of my dream of being a mother.

Hence, when women ask me if I have kids, I cringe emotionally and spiritually. I ache, and I want to cry. I know that God has forgiven my sin, but I still struggle mightily with forgiving myself.

After my abortion, I became severely depressed. I would cry randomly and inconsolably to the point of exhaustion. One night, at my sister's house, I couldn't stop crying for hours on end. I was crying so profusely that I was hyperventilating, and my body was shaking uncontrollably.

My sister kept begging me to stop crying because she was so concerned. She almost took me to the hospital. My biological sister,

Lisa, was ready to have me committed because she was sure I was having a nervous breakdown.

Somehow, I stopped crying, but then I just sat there mute, staring at nothing while thinking about everything. My soul was tortured. The self-inflicted trauma of my abortion proved too much for me to handle. That is what finally broke me. After all the other traumas I had suffered at the hands of others, it was my sin, not theirs, that ultimately destroyed me.

Shame and self-loathing had planted their roots in my soul. The soil of my soul was perfect, and the climate ideal to breed even more destruction in my life. The toxicity in my life continued to grow because my spiritual brokenness allowed it to thrive.

I hated myself and wanted my baby back. I was filled with every negative emotion you can think of, and there was no reprieve. I woke up in pain with immediate thoughts about what I had done and went to sleep with it as well.

Death had finally completely permeated my heart and soul. The pain was so intense that inevitably, I couldn't take it anymore, and that's when I started self-medicating with alcohol. I was twenty-seven years old when I began my journey of addiction. I had the same disease as my mother, and I had fallen into the same trap: I was an alcoholic. I can even remember the exact day I turned the corner, not the date itself, just everything I did and felt on that particular day.

I was working from my home office, but I couldn't concentrate on my work because I was severely depressed. Suddenly, I remembered that I had wine in the refrigerator and went to get it. It was roughly eleven o'clock in the morning, and I recall that distinctly because that gave me pause. It was so early in the day, and I never drank during the day.

My next thought was, *I live by myself; no one will know I drank this early. I'll only do it today.*

Anyone who struggles with addiction will tell you that is "addict thinking." Secrecy, lies, and deception are the soil in which addiction grows. The irony is that we don't just lie and deceive others. We do the same thing to ourselves.

As an addict, I began lying to myself immediately in an effort to pretend that all was well. I convinced myself that I had control over the disease that was starting to manifest. The guilt and shame grew slowly but started right away. I knew what I was doing was wrong, yet I validated my actions and behaviors. Sadly, soon enough, the mental obsession and physical compulsion started to set in.

I quickly learned how to get comfortable with being very uncomfortable. As I fell further and further into my addiction, I acclimated to the negative outcomes of my behaviors and decisions. I had no choice because as long as I was in active addiction, the toxic cycle would only continue. The alcohol, the bad behavior, and the consequences. On and on it went, and the worse it got. Addiction is a progressive disease. Alcoholics need more alcohol to get drunk, and the same goes for people who use drugs; they will need more to get high. In the twelve-step programs, we have a saying, "One is too many, and a thousand is never enough." That is the reality and burden of every person with an addiction.

The definition of insanity is doing the same thing over and over again and expecting a different result, and yet, that's what I did. I kept going back to the thing that was killing me and lied to myself by saying that next time, it would be different. The lie was an excuse to do it again, and I was very good at lying to myself.

Eventually, it occurred to me that my romantic relationships acted as previews of my relationship with alcohol. I learned to accept pain, self-disgust, and hopelessness with those men. My self-imposed prolonged exposure to those emotions caused me to develop an unhealthy tolerance for them.

However, I don't blame Ryan or Sal for my loss of self, not at all. They behaved the way they did, and I accepted it. The truth is that we teach people how to treat us. I had no boundaries with either man. I simply accepted anything they would give me, which was very little. Somehow, I convinced myself that the little I had of them was better than nothing at all.

Ultimately, it was a lack of love and respect for myself that caused me to stay and suffer horribly. They might have broken my heart, but I handed them the hammer. That was my part, which was a huge part, so I accept the blame.

Alcohol wound up becoming my best friend. I sought refuge with it, commiserated with it, and it didn't judge me. It numbed me, so I felt it made life more palatable until it didn't. Until it took over everything, including myself, and sought to kill me. That's when it became my worst enemy.

I entered my thirties convinced that I would get control over my drinking, but I never did. The longer I fed "the beast," the worse it got. I found that I needed more of the poison that was killing me. I didn't want to feel my emotional agony, so I sought oblivion with alcohol. Then, after drinking, I would feel defeated because I knew I needed to stop. However, I would infuriate myself because I would return to it again as a means of escape. Round and round, I went in an endless cycle of guilt, shame, frustration, depression, and anger.

The shame I felt about my disease only added fuel to the fire because I didn't want to admit that I had a problem. I feared judgment, so I wouldn't ask for help.

It was exhausting, utterly exhausting. It was also incredibly lonely. I can say that it was because the longer I drank, the more I chose to isolate myself.

Other than work and weekly dinners with my family, my social life mainly consisted of singing in the band that I was in. I sang in bars and clubs, and of course, that suited my alcoholic drinking perfectly. However, as much as I enjoyed singing, I wasn't in love with it anymore.

There were so many horrible consequences of my addiction. One of them was that I lost interest in the things I used to love. As my soul died, so did my desire to do things that brought me joy. It was a spiritual, emotional, mental, and physical death sentence. Some addicts die a slow death, while others meet their end very quickly.

There's no telling what they will face, but either way, it is horrible. It's no life; I can assure you of that. It's barely an existence.

I was in my mid-thirties and in the throes of my addiction when I wound up revisiting a relationship from my past. My ex-boyfriend James reached out to me via social media, and despite my many reservations, I agreed to see him.

I had quite a history with James because I dated him on and off during my relationship with Ryan. Unfortunately, James had suffered along with me because I would end things with him anytime Ryan wanted me back. James was always second fiddle; he was never first place with me. I loved him very much, but I was never in love with him. I now realize I had played with his heart like Ryan did with mine.

When James came back into my life, I was severely depressed and drinking heavily. Quite frankly, I couldn't care less about love or relationships. I was candid with James about my drinking and where I was, both emotionally and mentally. Surprisingly and shockingly, he accepted me as broken as I was and wanted to be with me.

Obviously, to start a relationship in such a manner is a recipe for disaster. Broken people make destructive decisions, and I was definitely broken. I chose to rekindle my childhood romance with James because I thought I didn't have to fear getting emotionally devastated by him, but I couldn't have been more wrong.

I was with James for almost two years, which was a lot longer than I think anyone expected. Romantically, we weren't a good match in any way, but we were great friends, that I can say. However, that is not enough in a romantic relationship and wasn't enough for either of us.

I was the sole provider during our time together, which made me extremely resentful. I'm ashamed to say that I became verbally abusive toward him because of it. It is true when they say, "Hurt people hurt people." I had so many wounds, and they bled all over James.

At that point, I didn't even recognize myself anymore. It felt like I had a monster inside me that I kept locked in Pandora's box, and the key to unleash it was alcohol. I know now that the "monster" was trauma and that all the horrible attributes it possessed were expressions of my profound pain. Trauma will always make itself heard and felt in some way, someday. My soul had been saturated with sorrow for so long that it had turned into wrath. So when I drank, the darkest shadow of myself, which I took great effort to hide, would come out.

In my early sobriety, when I was doing my step work, I made amends to James for my behavior. He forgave me and asked for forgiveness for his actions, but it still bothers me that I was so hurtful. When I apologized to James, he told me about things he had been struggling with, things he never disclosed while we were together, and we agreed that our relationship was doomed from the very start.

My relationship with James always had an element of volatility, even when we were kids. We both had tempers, and as much as we cared about each other, we just rubbed each other the wrong way. Fundamentally, we were incompatible. We looked at life very differently and frequently disagreed on things. We rarely came to the same conclusions about people or situations. So, in a sense, there was always some type of discord between us, even in our better times.

However, in our thirties, we were both in depressive and self-destructive seasons of our lives. My feelings were prominently displayed through my drinking, anger, and sorrow. Meanwhile, James's feelings presented themselves as a lack of motivation and participation in life. He was passively aggressive, and I was blatantly aggressive. It was a constant battle of wills because I wanted a partner I could lean on, and he wanted a partner who would take care of him in every way.

At first, my relationship with James seemed to be a good choice because I didn't have to hide how sick I was or how much I had changed. My life of addiction involved lying and trying to deceive everyone else because I didn't want them to see what I had become. There was a permanent mask that I wore as an addict, a character I played for the facade of a life that I lived. I constantly tried to convince people that all was well, and if I couldn't fool them anymore, I avoided them. At that time, the people who loved me and whom I loved represented mirrors that I couldn't bring myself to look at.

However, it wasn't that way with James. He was broken and dissatisfied with his life, although his traumas differed from mine, and he dealt with them in other ways.

When we dated as kids, James always had a job, sometimes multiple jobs, and helped support his family. He was quite a hustler when we were younger, and I had admired that about him. James seemed in control of his life and destiny then. However, as an adult, he seemed very content to let me be the sole provider and not contribute in any way. I was in a constant state of frustration, anger, and resentment, which then turned into a total lack of respect for him. I don't think he respected me either because he knew firsthand just how sick I was and what I'd been reduced to. I wasn't the vibrant, loving girl from his childhood. Instead, I was an angry, bitter, and depressed alcoholic. I was a broken woman with a broken heart who had given up on her dreams. I hated my life and who I had become, and James knew it.

When both people in a relationship are mentally, spiritually, and emotionally sick, nothing good can come of it. For me and James, what started as comfort ended in contempt.

Our fateful day started like any other, I suppose. My sister, Lisa, was having a barbeque, so James and I drove to her house to attend it. While there, I ran into my cousin, whom I hadn't spoken to in quite some time because of a falling out. James was fully aware of the fight we had and how hurt I had been, so he got agitated when he saw us reconciling. Later in the day, when he was forced to converse with her, he treated her rudely, and afterward, she mentioned it to me. I was so angry. No matter what problems James had within his family, I never acted unbecoming towards any of his family members. I was always cordial, respectful, and polite, even if I was displeased with them. James's behavior was inexcusable, and I told him as much. When I did, he made it clear that he could care less; he simply shrugged his shoulders and walked away from me. Then, I was livid.

After the barbecue ended, we headed home. We argued the entire ride back. After we got home, we weren't yelling at each other anymore, but we were both still angry. So we just gave each other the silent treatment and ignored each other for hours.

Eventually, I decided to go to bed because I had a job interview the next day. As I started walking towards our bedroom, James began to yell at me again, so I turned around and returned to the living room. I sat down on the couch as he ranted at me, telling me that I was stupid for reconciling with my cousin and that I would regret it. That's when I interrupted James and said that I only regretted getting back together with him and that I was stupid for allowing him back into my life because he added nothing of value to it.

Then, he snapped. I saw the murderous look on his face as he charged at me. Before I knew it, James had his hands around my throat and was strangling me. I couldn't breathe and kept trying to shove him off of me, but James was too strong. I also tried grabbing at his hands to pry them off of my neck, to no avail. The look on his face terrified me. There was so much hatred in his eyes but also a certainty that told me that he wanted to kill me and had decided to do so. Then, all of a sudden, James stopped. He took his hands off of my neck and stood up. In a later conversation with James, he told me that the look of absolute fear in my eyes stopped him.

As I sat there gasping for breath and coughing, I looked at him. I couldn't believe what had happened. Here was a man I had known since I was sixteen, with whom I had shared countless memories. James probably knew me better than anyone, and he just tried to kill me.

James sat across from me and tried apologizing, but I wasn't hearing it. Instead, my fear turned into rage, and I attacked him. It was the worst thing I could have done, but I had been drinking and couldn't control my emotions. That only infuriated James again, so he proceeded to throw me down on the floor and started kicking me. I screamed in pain and tried to get away, but I couldn't.

Thankfully, my next-door neighbors heard me and went to find the security guard posted in my apartment complex. After they told him what they heard, he came to my unit and let himself into my apartment with his key. By the time the security guard got inside and made his way up the stairs, James had stopped kicking me, but I was still on the floor. I was curled up in the fetal position, crying hysterically, and the security guard told James he had to leave.

I knew the security guard well because he would keep an eye out for me when I got home late from my gigs with the band. His name was Michael, and he was always kind enough to walk me to my door to ensure my safety.

That night, Michael told me that he would sit in front of my door until morning to make sure that James didn't come back. The look in his eyes spoke loudly of his concern for me. My bruises were already evident, and I was still crying hysterically. Michael looked around my ransacked apartment and sighed sadly. I lived in a second-story unit and followed him as he walked down the stairs. I told Michael he didn't have to sit there all night, but he wouldn't hear of it. So, I thanked him profusely and closed the door.

Once I locked the door, I just leaned on it and kept crying; then I started hyperventilating. I crawled back up the stairs because I felt like I could barely breathe and physically felt incapable of walking. I was completely shocked; my mind had trouble processing everything. I didn't call my parents because it was late and I was beyond exhausted. I also couldn't imagine how I would tell them about what happened. Then, I finally got into bed and fell asleep.

The next day, I woke up to my alarm, and despite all the pain I was in, I remembered that I had a job interview. So, I took a shower and proceeded to get ready. I covered the bruises on my neck with makeup and arranged my long hair strategically. I put on my suit and was thankful it covered all the other evidence of James's attack. I put on my professional persona like a second skin and wore my mask of calmness and control. I looked in the bathroom mirror to check my makeup and hated the broken woman looking back at me. So I stopped looking at her, tried to shake off my disgust, and left my apartment.

As I drove to the interview, I was in a daze. I felt like I was in a horrible dream that I couldn't wake up from. I wanted to turn around and go back home, but I wouldn't allow myself to because I needed a job desperately. So, I forced myself to be in the moment and remember the character I was supposed to play.

Once at the interview, I smiled and engaged appropriately. I was eloquent and portrayed confidence, so I got the job. All the tools and tricks of manipulation and deception that I learned from my life of addiction were utilized in that interview. The woman sitting in front of me had no clue that a battered woman was sitting in front of her. She had no idea that I had almost lost my life about ten hours earlier. When I think of my ability at that time to erect such a convincing facade after a life-threatening trauma, it boggles my mind. When I think back on that version of myself, especially on that particular day, I want to cry, which is what I did when I got back to my car afterward. I sat there for about fifteen minutes or so and cried hysterically. Then, I drove home and got drunk.

That is the perfect illustration of addiction. Someone had just tried to kill me, and the very next day, I went back to killing myself.

That is the absolute insanity of addiction. It is an insidious disease, and that's the reason so many people die because of it.

Later that same day, while drinking, I called my parents and sisters and told them what happened. However, I didn't anticipate my parents insisting I stay with them until I changed the locks on my apartment door. Had I known, I'd like to think that I wouldn't have started drinking, but my disease had already progressed significantly, so I highly doubt it.

By the time my father came to pick me up, I was drunk. I was horrified because my father had never seen me that way before. I had spoken to my parents on the phone several times while tipsy but avoided drinking around them as much as possible. The disappointment and disapproval on my father's face that day was more than I could bear, especially after what happened to me. I don't blame him, though; I'm sure I reminded him of my mother at that moment, which must have brought up many painful memories.

Once, during my recovery journey, my father told me, "For someone who's never had an issue with alcohol, it sure has affected my life." My heart broke for him when he said that because he was right. The disease of addiction has many victims.

My parents convinced me to call the police to report what happened, so I contacted them when I returned to my apartment. After I spoke with them, they sent a police officer to take my statement. When he arrived, he said that I had waited too long to report the incident and that nothing would come of it because there was no proof of what had transpired. That's when I moved my hair to show him the bruises on my neck. When the officer saw them, he looked shocked, and then I pulled up my sleeves to show him the bruises on my arms. He asked, "Didn't this incident occur five days ago?" and I said, "Yes." That's when he said, "And your bruises are still this bad?"

At that point, the police officer insisted on coming into my apartment. He walked up the stairs, and when he reached the top, he saw the mess in my living room from James's attack on me. I had gotten home only an hour prior, so I had no time to clean up. Then, the officer sat down at my dining room table and wrote a report about everything that had taken place, which took well over an hour. Once finished, he told me that other officers would drop by later to follow up. I had no idea what that would entail, but I would soon find out.

A couple of hours later, the other officers arrived and took pictures of me and my apartment. They had me stand there and show them all the bruises on my neck, arms, legs, and back while they took pictures for evidence. I felt vulnerable and humiliated. I know they were just doing their jobs, so I don't blame them, but as a woman, I felt entirely exposed, which made me feel violated.

Little did I know that in the state of New York, it is the state that presses charges after a domestic violence incident, not the victim. James got arrested later that week.

I changed even further after that ordeal. I drank more to forget what happened, but I couldn't. I was mortified that my father had seen me in such a state. I couldn't believe what had happened or that I was a victim of domestic violence. Of all the roles I imagined I would play in my life, that one was certainly not on the list. The incident with James and the aftermath of it was defining for me. It perfectly represented what my life had become, the chaos that was me and my world.

> *As water reflects the face, so one's life reflects the heart.*
> Proverbs 27:19 (NIV)

I left the band I was in a few months later. I couldn't sing anymore, not physically, but emotionally. I had nothing to give to music. It was no longer my joy, therapy, or sanctuary, as it had been my entire life. My power to create had vanished, and I knew it. I was filled with immense pain, and where there wasn't pain, there was an excruciating emptiness. I couldn't create when I felt like I was barely existing.

While it might not seem significant in the scheme of things, it was very telling. As I mentioned earlier, addiction will steal anything from the addict that brings them joy. It will steal all their hopes and dreams. It also will rob them of their family and friends. It wants to kill and destroy everything, and when there's nothing else left, it seeks to kill the addict, too.

Stage 3

The Painful Pupa (Chrysalis)

I only survived my thirties because I loved my cats like they were my children. In fact, I never called them my cats; I always called them my babies. Their names were Derek, Maxi, and Sophie, and they saved me day after day because they loved me when I didn't love myself. They gave my life meaning because caring for them gave me some sense of self-worth. It mattered to them if I lived or died when it didn't matter to me at all. The only true happiness I derived from my life was being their mommy, and I loved to spoil my babies in any way I could. They always comforted me with their displays of unconditional love and devotion; there were many because my babies were very sweet and affectionate. They would rarely leave my side, and I desperately needed that companionship. I can not stress it enough when I say that I wouldn't have made it to my forties without them.

I moved to Florida with them a few weeks before my fortieth birthday. Some of my family had begun relocating there, and they were very nervous at the thought of me living in New York alone. Initially, I was offended and told them as much, but afterward, I realized they were right. Besides, after everything that happened to me in New York, I thought it best that I move somewhere else to start over.

I was extremely excited about moving because I thought I could leave all my problems behind. However, I was still an active alcoholic, so the biggest piece of baggage I carried with me was my addiction. Alcoholism is a progressive disease, which means that the disease only gets worse, and so does the addict. I was no exception, so there was no way that my troubles would be left behind in New York. I was only deluding myself.

I drove down to Florida with my biological sister, Lisa, and my babies; it was a very chaotic trip. My cat Derek, "Papa," as I called him, was "cat crying" almost the entire car ride to voice his objections. He didn't like the car, and he didn't like being in the carrier. He was eighteen pounds and a Mama's boy. Derek's capacity for love was even larger than his frame. I had Derek since he was a kitten; he was my first feline baby, the love of my life, and we had never been on a trip like this before.

Then there was my baby boy Maxi, who I called "Doodle Baby." He was the second cat I got because Derek needed a playmate. He was incredibly sweet and loving but was an anxious cat because his first owners abused him. When I got Maxi, Derek welcomed and comforted him on his first night with us, so Maxi was extremely attached to his big brother. Maxi's anxiety worsened when he was confined to small spaces, and he hated being apart from Derek, so Maxi used his teeth and nails to rip open the mesh on his carrier and climbed out mid-trip! That prompted my sister to pull over the car and for me to sit in the back seat with them all, which was a tight fit.

Throughout all the commotion, my beautiful, feisty baby girl Sophie was as quiet as a mouse. She stayed almost perfectly still during the entire ride down to Florida, and while some people would think she was composed, as her mother, I knew she was scared.

When we finally got to our new apartment in Florida, I let them all out of their carriers, and they were so relieved! So was I, for that matter. Despite the hectic and chaotic car ride down, I felt freer and freer the further we got from New York. I loved my home state but couldn't wait to leave. I was ready to start a new life and was convinced that Florida was the answer to all my problems. However, as they say, "Wherever you go, there you are." Simply put, I couldn't escape myself or my alcoholism, no matter where I went.

During the drive down to Florida, my sister mentioned my drinking. She, more than anyone else, had to deal with my erratic behavior when I was drunk. Unfortunately, Lisa was often the recipient of the anger and disgust I felt about my life. I honestly can't count how many times I had to apologize to her the next morning after calling her in a rage about whatever had come into my inebriated mind the night before.

Lisa suggested that I seek help for my alcoholism. She thought it would be the perfect time to do so because Florida would be a new beginning for me. So, to end the uncomfortable conversation, I told her I would think about it.

After I had settled into my new apartment, I went to work for my sister Lisa and her husband. They had moved their business from New York to Florida and encouraged my parents to move to the Sunshine State as well. My sister Lisa and her husband had been married for many years, and while my sister wanted me to work for them, he did not.

Throughout my life, from the earliest of ages, my sister Lisa and I had more of a maternal/daughter relationship than that of sisters. It started when my mother had custody of us, and she was unable to care for me. My sister would frequently change my diapers and feed me. She was always under strict instructions from my mother to "take care of the baby." Even as I got older, my sister always felt compelled to care for me to the best of her ability, which was a heavy burden. One that she was first asked to carry while she was just a baby herself. It was unfair to Lisa, and I feel horrible that she had to grow up so quickly. Unfortunately, it also cultivated a very co-dependent relationship between us. Our motto was, "You and me against the world." Sadly, we have known how difficult life can be since childhood and have always been determined to face it together.

At first, I thoroughly enjoyed working for my sister and her husband, but underlying tensions were always at play. I knew her husband didn't want me there, and I resented that because he had family members who worked for them. So, I always thought, *What is his problem with me working here?*

In retrospect, I realized that my alcoholism was probably a huge concern for him. I also think he was worried about the dynamic of my relationship with my sister. Perhaps he thought she couldn't be my boss effectively. Unfortunately, I chose not to understand his feelings; instead, I was just resentful of them. I also got jealous of the friendships my sister cultivated with his family. I didn't feel like a priority in my sister's life anymore, but I know now that I was being incredibly self-centered and immature.

> *Anger is cruel and fury overwhelming, but who can stand before jealousy?*
>
> Proverbs 27:4 (NIV)

It took quite some time, but I eventually decided to get help for my drinking. However, I didn't make that decision because I was ready to. I only made it to please Lisa and strengthen our relationship. I didn't like sharing my sister with all of her new friends in Florida and believed if I got sober, I would no longer have to.

So, I walked into Lisa's office one morning and told her I wanted to find a twelve-step meeting. She had been looking at her computer when I made the announcement, but as soon as she realized what I said, her head snapped up. Lisa looked at me with wide eyes; her face radiated shock and joy. Immediately, she searched the internet and found a local place that held twelve-step meetings.

A few days later, I attended my first meeting with Lisa by my side. It felt like old times. I felt the familiar weight of my sister's hand in mine, and it soothed me. In my selfish mind, all was right with the world because Lisa's attention was completely focused on me and my needs.

I went to meetings nearly every day for two months and remained sober during that time. However, only a few days after I had achieved sixty days of sobriety, I drank again. I made that horrible choice because I had gotten sober for my sister, not for myself.

It didn't take Lisa long to figure out that I began drinking again, and when she did, she was extremely disappointed. I tried desperately to convince her and myself that two months of recovery was all I needed. I told her I wasn't as sick as everyone else in the meetings, so I didn't belong there. That was a lie, of course, but as I mentioned earlier, I was very good at lying to myself.

When I first started drinking again, I drank a lot less, but unfortunately, that didn't last for long. Before I knew it, I was drinking even more than I had before my short-lived recovery. My disease was on the move again, and it seemed like it was determined to make up for lost time.

My relationship with Lisa only got more estranged after she discovered that I was drinking again, which made things even more uncomfortable for me at work. At first, it was just her husband who didn't want me there, but then I started to feel like Lisa didn't want me there either.

My feelings of resentment towards my sister and my discomfort at the job only continued to grow as time went on. I wound up working for them for over three years but never looked for another job. Instead, I stayed because it was easier than striking out on my own.

Then, one day, I made a mistake on a large purchase order. When it came to light, I was suspended for three days without pay. To say I was livid doesn't even begin to describe how I felt. It was as if I was the incarnation of wrath. Self-righteous anger, bitterness, and a very wounded ego fueled my ferocious fire.

I left the office after I got suspended and drove straight to the store to pick up multiple bottles of wine. I proceeded to go on a five-day bender. Sadly, those initial bottles didn't last me long; I returned at least twice to get more. I quickly drank more than twelve big bottles of wine during that spree and felt physically and emotionally sick when I finally returned to work.

The entire time I was drinking, I kept thinking about quitting. Logically, I knew I needed the job, but my pride said differently. So I quit. Dramatically, I'm embarrassed to say. When I returned to work, they said I needed to sign off on paperwork regarding my suspension, but I refused to. Then I told them I was quitting, but not before I said a few choice words.

> *My dear brothers and sisters, take note of this: Everyone should be quick to listen, slow to speak and slow to become angry, because human anger does not produce the righteousness that God desires.*
>
> James 1:19-20 (NIV)

Quitting caused significant problems within my family. We weren't raised to behave that way, but unfortunately, I had lost myself to alcohol long before that incident, so I had what can only be described as an emotional explosion. My father was infuriated with me because I had embarrassed him with my behavior and hurt my sister. He refused to speak to me. Anytime I called the house, my stepmother, Evelyn, would answer the phone and talk to me, but he wouldn't. Also, I wasn't going to family dinner every week anymore because if I was there, my sister didn't want to be, so everything became very strained. That only made me drink more.

Once again, I had the sickening feeling in my soul of being unwanted. It was the horrible familiar feeling of my youth, only now it wasn't my mother; it was my father. I felt expendable all over again.

My best friend, Alicia, lived in North Carolina, and I told her what happened. After hearing the whole story, she suggested I move by her. So I did. I packed my clothes and fur babies, left my furniture and family behind, and hit the road. I tried to convince myself that my life would be better in North Carolina. It was the typical tale I told myself, that things would be better somewhere else. I would never admit that my problem was not about location but addiction.

It was great spending time with my best friend. We hadn't lived close to each other in years, so seeing her in person, rather than speaking only on the phone, was wonderful. I always got along with her husband and considered her two boys my nephews. So, in essence, her family became mine while I was there. It felt like they adopted me, and for that, I was grateful. Alicia even helped me get a job at the bank where she worked. It was only a temporary assignment, but I was enthusiastic because it was a start. Slowly but surely, my life began to take shape there, but my heart and soul were still profoundly distressed.

Eventually, I did get a permanent full-time job. It wasn't ideal because I couldn't stand what I was selling, but it was a paycheck. However, my drinking only continued to get worse. After I paid my bills and got my babies what they needed, I would spend the rest of my money on wine. I didn't even buy furniture for my apartment. My friend Alicia was kind enough to give me her old mattress, so I slept on that. She also gave me one of her old couch cushions, which helped because it allowed me to sit on something other than my hard living room floor. Other than those two things and my TV, I had nothing.

My apartment was void of furniture but not of empty wine bottles. There were many scattered around my living room. I threw the remaining bottles into garbage bags and stuffed them into my cabinets and closet. I couldn't bring myself to throw them out because I was afraid my neighbors would hear them rattling in the garbage bags. I worried they would figure out that I was an alcoholic. They probably wouldn't have cared if they did find out, and I shouldn't have been concerned about it either way, but I was. I always cared about what everyone else thought because I didn't think much of myself.

I suffered enormous anxiety about the state of my apartment. My greatest fear was that management would come inside and see how I was living. I wish my fear would have motivated me to do something about it, but it never did. Instead, I had what is called "Analysis Paralysis". I would analyze the situation and try to devise a plan of action, but ultimately, I would get completely overwhelmed by the enormity of what needed to be done. I would look at the mess and hate it, but I couldn't bring myself to do anything about it.

Eventually, I spoke to my best friend Alicia about my apartment and its appearance. I always went over to her house, so she hadn't seen my place since shortly after I had moved in. When Alicia found out, she said she was coming over and wasted no time. She left her children with her husband and immediately drove to my place.

When Alicia walked inside, she just stood there, stunned. I actually had to tell her to close the door. Then she started to cry, and Alicia rarely cries. She looked at the bottles and then at me and said, "Nina, are you trying to kill yourself?"

I replied, "Yes."

Then, she stopped crying and said, "Sit down. We need to talk."

I gave her the couch cushion and sat on the floor. My shoulders were slumped in defeat as I stared at the floor. Then, I started crying.

After I finally stopped crying, Alicia said, "Look at me, Nina," but I didn't want to look at her because I was disgusted and embarrassed about what I'd been reduced to. I had been living in self-imposed squalor because my disease had progressed dramatically; I was extremely ill. Every night I went to bed, I wondered if I would wake up in the morning. Most nights, I can honestly say that I didn't care one way or another if I did.

I finally raised my head and forced myself to look into her eyes. Thankfully, Alicia could see how fragile I was, so she chose her words carefully. She began by telling me how much she loved me, saying that I was like a sister to her, but also said that she didn't understand why I hated myself. My best friend, one of the strongest women I know, said she was scared for me.

It's challenging to explain the disease of addiction to someone who doesn't have it because almost nothing we do makes sense. My actions and emotions weren't logical because I wasn't functioning from that space. The mental obsession and physical compulsion I experienced in active addiction dominated my life. Every waking moment, I wanted an alcoholic drink in my hand. If I wasn't drinking, I was thinking about when I could drink next. Every single decision I made was from a place of destruction and devastation. Addiction is prolonged torture of the mind, body, and soul. It's torture that the addict chooses, but let me be clear: we don't feel like we have a choice.

It took me and Alicia almost three hours to get my apartment cleared out and cleaned up. I was so relieved when we were finally done. I was also beyond grateful that I had an amazing friend who loved me enough to help me with something of that magnitude. Afterward, she told me she would come over occasionally to ensure I didn't let it get that way anymore. As embarrassing as that was, I agreed that she should because I didn't trust myself not to let it happen again. The state of my apartment reflected my emotional and mental state. My life was a mess, so my living space was as well. Caring about mundane things like cleaning and chores is almost impossible when you don't care about yourself.

A friend loves at all times, and a brother is born for a time of adversity.

Proverbs 17:17 (NIV)

As much as I wanted things to be better in North Carolina, they never were. My alcoholism had progressed to the point where I had resigned myself to the fact that it would kill me sooner or later.

Unfortunately, not every addict recovers, although I sincerely wish we all did. Sadly, some of us will never take another sober breath before we die. However, there is one constant: before we get sober, we hit what is called our bottom. There's no telling what the defining incident or incidents will be. Not even the addict knows beforehand what will ultimately break them.

For me, my bottom came in stages over several months. My surrender was slow and agonizing.

I was living in North Carolina for a little over a year when tragedy struck, and my bottom began. It started like any other day; I woke up hungover and went into the kitchen to put out fresh food and water for my babies. Then, I went to their litter box to clean it.

As bad as I always felt in the morning, I loved how excited they got about our routine! Derek would immediately start chattering away because he was the most vocal, and I would talk back to him like I understood what he was saying with all his meows and little chirps. While Derek and I would have our "conversation," Maxi would run to the dry food to eat it first, and Sophie would use the clean litter box before her brothers could get to it. Then later, when I left for work, I would stop at the door, turn around to look at them, and say, "Be good babies; don't be fresh babies! I love you, Derek! I love you, Maxi! I love you, Sophie!"

When I got home that night after work, my boys, Derek and Maxi, were waiting for me. They began meowing as soon as I walked in, so

I gave them their treats and pulled out my wine. Then, I sat down and started to watch TV while I drank. Everything seemed normal.

Unfortunately, it took me about forty-five minutes to realize that my baby girl, Sophie, hadn't come out. Sometimes, she would lag behind the boys, but never for that long, so I became concerned. Just as I was about to get up to look for her, I saw something out of the corner of my eye. It was Sophie, standing in the hallway. I looked at her and saw that her eyes were open wide in fear, and her mouth was hanging open. She was breathing erratically. I heard it clearly, and my next thought was that I was going to lose her. I don't know why that felt like a certainty to me, but it did. However, as soon as that thought crossed my mind, I shook my head, almost as if trying to physically expel the negative thought out of my mind.

I had the number of a local emergency vet on my phone, so I called them and told the receptionist about Sophie's condition. She told me to bring her in immediately and that they would see her as soon as I arrived.

Once I got off the phone, I started speaking to Sophie incessantly; I wouldn't shut up. I kept telling her I loved her and that she would be okay, but every time I looked at her, it scared me even more. I cried as I put her in the carrier and begged her to hang on as I ran out of my apartment.

When I got into my car, it dawned on me that I had been drinking, but Sophie was suffering, so I drove anyway. It was only a short drive to the vet, but time seemed to move so slowly. With every minute that passed, I worried that she wouldn't make it.

When I got there, I ran inside and spoke to the receptionist. After I reminded her of our phone call, she grabbed Sophie's carrier and raced to the back so the vet could tend to her. They were wonderful about taking care of her quickly, but they were terrible regarding the paperwork because they wanted me to fill out a ridiculous amount. They insisted that the paperwork be completed before I could see her, which frustrated me greatly. I wanted to be with my baby girl because she needed me.

A technician ran in as I finished the paperwork and told me I needed to see Sophie immediately. So I ran behind her into the next room, but it was too late. Sophie was gone. My beautiful baby girl lay lifeless on the examination table as the vet stood there with another technician. I felt grief starting to choke me. My throat and chest felt tight with sorrow. Then my sadness turned to anger because I was livid that I wasn't with her when she passed.

Yelling loudly, I told them both to leave the room, and they did. After they left, I scooped my little girl up in my arms and carried her like a baby. I walked around the room as I held her and kissed her little face. I kept apologizing that I hadn't been there with her when she needed me the most. Then I sat down and stared at her as I cried. My tears fell on Sophie as I tried to process everything that happened. I couldn't believe she was gone.

After I sat there a while, a technician came in and asked if I wanted my carrier back.

I couldn't believe she was asking me about a carrier while I was holding the lifeless body of my baby girl in my arms! So, I leveled her with a look that told her I wasn't pleased with her question and said, "No, you can keep it. I don't want it."

When I finally did get up from the chair, it felt like I had aged ten years. Then, I walked out of the room to find an employee. Once I did, I told her that I wanted Sophie cremated by herself. Then I handed Sophie's body to her and left the facility.

I drove home in shock because I couldn't understand what had happened. They said it was her heart, that she must have had some sort of defect. They had even tried giving her oxygen, but it didn't work. They were as baffled as I was because she was so young. Sophie was my youngest baby; she was only ten years old when she died.

She was my tiny jet-black princess. Everyone who met her commented on her beauty because Sophie was stunning. She was also fierce when she wanted to be and enjoyed intimidating her brothers. However, Sophie could also be very loving. Once, when Derek got sick, she wouldn't leave his side. Sophie lay beside him daily to comfort him until he got well. Afterward, she resumed her tough girl role with him, but Derek knew it was all an act. He still respected Sophie enough to cater to her mood swings and give her space when she wanted it, but he was no longer scared of her. I knew he would miss her very much once he realized she was gone.

As I drove, I kept replaying memories of my little girl. Sophie was my foster fail. I was supposed to be her foster mommy until she found a permanent home, but she stole my heart, and I couldn't give her up. I loved how Sophie used to sleep: she would sleep on her back with her paws in the air. It was beyond adorable. I also loved how her tail would quiver uncontrollably whenever I walked through the door after being out of the house. These were the images I kept seeing in my mind's eye as I drove; all I could see was her beautiful little face.

When I finally got home, my boys were waiting for me. They were confused when I came in without Sophie, so they started looking around for her. Utterly exhausted, I sat down on the floor and started crying again. Then, I picked up my bottle of wine and proceeded to drink straight out of it. I didn't even bother with a cup because my goal was to find oblivion, and I wanted to get there quickly.

When I got up the next morning, I called into work and took the day off. I told them I was sick, and I was, but it wasn't from a hangover; it was from my grief. The only productive thing I did that day was feed my boys and clean their litter box. After I took care of them, I went back to bed and cried myself to sleep. When I finally woke up again, I drank until I ran out of wine. Then, I went back to bed until I woke up for work the following day.

After several days, the boys stopped looking for Sophie, but I found that I couldn't stop looking for her. I kept expecting her to walk into the room or rub against my leg. I'd look for her in my bed when I woke up and then remember why she wasn't there. Sorrow kept hitting me in waves, and it wouldn't stop. The boys had finally accepted her absence, but I could not.

I had lived in a perpetual state of depression since the age of twenty-seven, and Sophie's death deepened it. I didn't want to do anything but drink and sleep. I wasn't eating much either because I didn't want food interfering with me getting drunk. It also didn't help matters that I could barely hold down food anymore and would frequently throw up what little I ate. I also started coughing up blood in the morning, which scared me but didn't stop me from consuming what was killing me.

When I finally got Sophie's ashes, I started sleeping with the box under my pillow. I would sleep with her box of ashes under my pillow every night until the last night I drank.

I wasn't functioning well at work at all. My sales were terrible because I just didn't care anymore. Usually, fear ruled me at work. I would work hard so I wouldn't get fired because I wanted to take care of my babies, but I didn't even have the energy to be fueled by fear anymore. I was utterly exhausted in every way: physically, mentally, and emotionally. As for my spiritual state, I was way past exhausted; I was bankrupt.

That's how I lived and felt for the next five months. Then, I woke up one Monday morning and decided that I didn't want to feel that way anymore; I decided to kill myself.

After I did, I immediately texted my boss and quit my job. I was weirdly relieved at the thought of what I would do. I had been trying to escape myself and my life for so many years, and nothing had worked, but I found comfort in the fact that killing myself would. I was convinced that it was the only way I could get rid of the pain that seemed to have embedded itself into the very marrow of my bones.

I decided that I was going to go to a hotel to live out my last days. I didn't want anyone to know where I was or what I was going to do. Then, once I ran out of money, I was going to drive somewhere to kill myself in my car using carbon monoxide. I planned to have my two boys in the back seat of my car because I didn't want to leave them without their mommy.

I packed a few things, put the boys in their carriers, and headed to a local hotel. The week I spent there was torturous. All I did was cry and drink. I kept watching my boys, Derek and Maxi, thinking to myself that they had no clue as to what I was going to do. I stared at them often during our final days but took solace in the thought that we would die together.

On November 15, 2017, I left the hotel with our deaths in mind. Grief, shame, remorse, and sorrow have permanently etched that day in my memory. It was the third darkest day of my life. The first was the day I got the abortion, the second was the day my mother Carmen died, and the third was the day I sentenced my baby boys to their deaths. However, there was a very significant difference between those days. The death of my mother was something I couldn't control, while the others were consequences of my horrible choices. The profound remorse I feel in my heart and soul regarding those choices is solely owned by me. I am responsible. I have no one else to blame but myself.

It was a gloomy day, as I remember it. Although the sun could have shone brightly with glorious rainbows in the sky, and it wouldn't have mattered. I wouldn't have seen or felt it and certainly wouldn't have acknowledged it. All I could think of was the fact that I had my two baby boys in my car, so I could drive them to a high-kill shelter and give them up after fourteen years together.

For the first time in my life, no one knew where I was, which was what I wanted. I no longer wanted to live and didn't want to discuss it with anyone. As I explained, I planned to kill myself in my car along with my two boys. However, when I thought long and hard about it, I felt they would somehow sense what I would do. Maybe they would smell the carbon monoxide I planned to fill my car with to kill us all, and they would start crying in fear. I knew I couldn't die hearing that, and I wouldn't be able to go through with killing myself if I did, so I decided to bring them to a high-kill shelter. It pains me that I saw no other options, but I truly felt that there weren't any at that time. The constant emotional agony and mental anguish were unbearable. I was as miserable and depressed as I imagine any person is right before taking their own life.

The boys were both upset because we were in the car again. In the fourteen years we had spent together, they had never traveled that much with me in the car. They were only accustomed to quick trips to and from the vet. I felt like they were losing patience with me and trust in me. Not that I blamed them. Their fierce loyalty had been tested one too many times.

I dreaded the next part of our seemingly endless journey. I never moved so slowly in my life or cried more frequently. I was petrified at the thought of what I was going to do to myself and horrified by what I was going to do to them, but I was resigned. An unrelenting feeling of hopelessness had consumed me. I desperately wanted to wake up from the nightmare that was my life, but I knew I wasn't sleeping. This was the bleak reality of my existence. This was where my addiction brought me, and death was the only choice I thought I had.

As I drove the car, I visualized what the world would look like without me in it, and I'm very sad to say that I thought it would look a lot better. That was what my mind's eye saw, but unfortunately, addicts don't see well at all.

When I was in active addiction, I only saw the pain in front of me, and when I got tired of looking at that, I would replay painful memories from my past. I never saw possibilities or opportunities because I lived in a world of darkness. I never knew peace because I lived in a world of destruction and despair. I hated everything and everyone because I hated myself and my life. At that time, I wasn't a big fan of God either because I blamed Him for every bad thing that ever happened to me. I refused to accept ownership of my terrible life. I always looked outward to find blame instead of looking inward to take responsibility.

I finally found my way to the shelter and parked my car. I turned around to look at my two boys in their carriers. I told them how much I loved them but felt like a fraud. I felt like the worst person and infinitely the worst mother in the world because I knew Derek and Maxi's fate, and on some level, though it might seem absurd, I felt they knew it as well. Animals are highly sensitive creatures, and I believe that they have souls. Their souls in that moment and the following moments were in turmoil, as was mine. They felt my pain and anguish and adopted it as their own, as they often did with me over the years. However, this was different, and I believe they knew it was. They seemed to sense the end of our journey. While my big boy Derek looked depressed and defeated, my baby boy Maxi was filled with anxiety and confusion. Both of their reactions devastated me and only made me resign even further to killing myself later after I left them.

I finally walked inside. I had my boys in their respective carriers, and I spoke to a female employee about surrendering them. She advised me against it because they were senior cats and wouldn't have a good chance of getting rescued, but I insisted that I had to leave them there. She looked extremely disappointed when I said that, and I fully understood why.

However, that employee had no idea that she was speaking to a woman at the end of her rope who had already planned her suicide.

She thought she was talking to a person of sound mind, but she wasn't. I watched as she put them in separate cages. I asked if they could be kept together because they had never been apart, but she said, "No."

As I walked out of the room, I heard Maxi crying, and I thought my heart would burst with the pain it felt. I didn't know I could hate myself any more than I already did, but I was wrong.

If there had been a physical manifestation of all the sorrow and shame that I felt as I left the shelter, I would have bled out in the parking lot. I never would have even made it back to my car. I don't know how I managed to put one foot in front of the other. I'm shocked that I didn't collapse right outside that building.

When I did get to my car, I cried inconsolably, wailing like a tortured animal, and pounded my fists against my dashboard until I bruised myself. I didn't care that people around me were staring at me with frightened eyes because of my insanity. I didn't care because I was entirely engulfed by grief. I finally drove my car away and began screaming at myself. I called myself a murderer. I reminded myself over and over again that I had killed my unborn child and now had sentenced my baby boys to their deaths.

A part of me died when I left them there that day, and I know it's a part of me that I'll never get back. To this day, there is still a void in my heart where their unconditional love once lived.

I kept driving until I found a place to park where I thought I wouldn't be bothered. I wanted no witnesses to my death and didn't want anyone stopping me. I was resolute in my decision.

However, God is with us wherever we go, and He was definitely with me that day. As I was waiting for night to fall, my phone rang. It was an old friend of mine from Florida named Rose. We were very good friends at one point, but unfortunately, when I moved to North Carolina, I neglected the friendship. So, to say that I was surprised by the phone call, especially the timing of it, would be a massive understatement. I should also mention that she was a devout Christian.

I was still crying hysterically. Rose asked me what was going on, and I told her about my babies, what I did to them, and what I was getting ready to do to myself. She cried and begged me to reconsider. She told me that was the devil talking to me and implored me not to do anything until she called me back. I promised her I would wait ten minutes, but nothing more than that.

Unbeknownst to me, she contacted my biological sister, Lisa, through Facebook. They had never spoken to one another before that day, and my sister is very rarely on Facebook, but God makes the impossible possible. I hadn't spoken to my sister for months, but she called me back ten minutes later. Lisa spoke to me urgently, trying desperately to make her words reach me through my haze of insanity. Somehow, I heard her, and I listened. I can only attribute that to the fact that I had a lifetime of experience listening to and following my sister's directives. As the younger sibling, that was the role I was used to playing, and playing that role on that particular night saved my life.

My sister sent me money to rent a cheap motel room where I could stay the night and said she wanted me to come back to Florida the next day. Lisa said we would figure the rest out as a family when I returned. I couldn't comprehend what she meant by that or what that would entail, but I couldn't understand much of anything. Normally an intelligent woman, I was reduced to a hysterical, volatile, completely broken human being. I felt like I was shattered into a thousand pieces, so fragmented that I didn't think they could be put back together to resemble anything whole.

Lisa sent the money through Walmart and found one online near where I had parked. She gave me the address and told me to call her back once I picked it up. I drove there slowly, in a fog of disbelief. I wasn't even sure what was happening was real, but that was probably because I didn't want it to be. I finally found the Walmart, but because of my confusion, what should have been a fifteen-minute drive turned into a half hour.

I walked inside and headed straight to Customer Service because I was supposed to pick up the money transfer there. When I got to the counter, I saw a young lady behind it and told her what I was there for. She looked at me apologetically and said that service was no longer available because I had arrived after their cut-off time. According to their rules, she wasn't allowed to give me the money, so she suggested I return when the store reopened in the morning. I told her that I would and thanked her for her help. Dejected, I started walking away. I also began mentally preparing myself to sleep in my car until morning.

Then, something happened that I can only attribute to God interceding on my behalf once again. The young girl called out to me, saying, "Ma'am! Please come back!"

So, I turned around and headed back to the counter. Once I got there, she stared at me for a long moment and said, "Hold on, I'm going to give you your money."

I looked at her in shock and replied, "But won't you get in trouble?"

She paused and said, "Yes, I will, but I'll worry about that. I'm giving you your money."

I was rendered speechless for a minute as I watched her turn the machine she needed to use back on. Then I said, "God is going to bless you abundantly for doing this because you're helping one of His children. You have no idea what this means to me or how much I needed your kindness today. Thank you so much."

She looked at me with a soft, slightly sad smile and said, "I could really use some blessings."

With absolute sincerity and what felt like certainty in my soul, I told her, "God is definitely going to bless you. Believe me."

Then she smiled, but her smile wasn't sad anymore, it was happy and expectant.

After she gave me the money, I left the store and walked to my car. I called my sister and told her I had the money and would look for a nearby motel. After I got off the phone, I sat in the car for several minutes, reflecting on what happened. I was still shocked by the young lady's actions. The selflessness she displayed for a stranger was astonishing, and that is what I was to her: a stranger. I was also stunned by what I said to her. I couldn't believe I told her that God would bless her or that I had referred to myself as one of His children. I had been running from God for such a long time and most certainly didn't want to acknowledge that I was His child during that time. So, I wondered, *Why did those words come out of my mouth?* I knew when I said them that I meant them, but as I sat in the car, I was still baffled by the words that had passed from my lips.

In hindsight, and because of my relationship with God now, I know why I said those things. I said them because intuitively, I knew that God was with us at that moment. He had moved her heart to show me compassion, and afterward, the Lord let me know that He would bless her for her good deed. That's what I believe happened. It wasn't a financial transaction, at least not in God's eyes. It was a spiritual one.

> *So do not fear, for I am with you; do not be dismayed,*
> *for I am your God. I will strengthen you and help you;*
> *I will uphold you with my righteous right hand.*
>
> Isaiah 41:10 (NIV)

I finally left the parking lot and drove around until I found a motel sign. Once I did, I paid for a room and got the key. When I walked inside the room, I saw how dingy and dirty it looked, but I didn't care because it seemed to suit me. I was disgusted with it, but I was disgusted with myself, so what did it matter? I had my old familiar friend, my wine with me, and I went to drink it, but I only drank a little. Then I slammed the bottle down, pushed it away from me, and screamed at it. I yelled, "You can't even do what I need you to do for me!"

That was the first time in seventeen years of addiction that I knew the alcoholic anesthesia wouldn't work. I knew it wouldn't have the capability of relieving the excruciating, heartbreaking, and soul-shattering pain that I felt. It couldn't do it. I knew that, and I was furious, but that moment defined my sobriety to come. I was forced to face life on life's terms, without altering myself and without desperately trying to find an escape.

November 15, 2017, was a defining day in my life. It forced me to seek death or seek recovery. I had to decide to live or die. Thankfully, I chose to live, even though I didn't feel worthy and wouldn't for quite some time. However, the emotional death of my former self was the catalyst for my rebirth.

I'm eternally grateful for the phone call from my friend, the next call from my sister, and, ultimately, the call I received from God.

> *The Lord is close to the brokenhearted and saves those who are crushed in spirit.*
>
> Psalm 34:18 (NIV)

On November 16, 2017, my sobriety date, I got in my car and drove back to Florida to be with my family. The trip took me a little over seven hours, and all I kept thinking about was going to rehab, which was shocking because I had never wanted to go prior. I even said it out loud, like a mantra; I repeated one simple sentence throughout my journey back home. I said, "Please let them send me to rehab."

I didn't realize at the time that it was my first prayer to God in sobriety. I also did not know that He would answer that prayer almost immediately.

When I got back home to my parents' house, they told me that they wanted me to go to rehab, and I remember being stunned because they had never said that before. They were even more amazed when I quickly agreed to go. I had no money or health insurance, so my parents paid for it. It was quite expensive, but that wasn't their focus at all. All they were concerned about was me. My parents wanted to get me the help I needed. They also understood that they were out of their depths as parents because they didn't suffer from my disease. If you don't have the disease of addiction, it is incredibly hard to comprehend what it does to the mind, body, and soul, and they were wise enough to know that. Over the next few days, my parents took me to two different rehab facilities, and we collectively decided which one I would go to.

My road to recovery started when I left North Carolina and began driving back home. I knew I needed my family's help, but I finally conceded that I would also need professional help. That was the most significant and crucial step I've made in my recovery because it bridged the enormous gap between who I was and who I wanted to be. It was the bridge of hope; I realize that now. For only hope will allow us to imagine a better tomorrow and better life.

But now, Lord, what do I look for? My hope is in you.

Psalm 39:7 (NIV)

In the final stage of a caterpillar's life, it becomes a butterfly. The caterpillar's painful journey ultimately leads to an extraordinary transformation. That is when we finally see its beauty, which is exactly what happened to me. My life's most transformative and beautiful stage was born from great pain. That is the next chapter you will read of my story, and it is the one I am still living today.

Stage 4

A Beautiful Butterfly

He has made everything beautiful in its time. He has also set eternity in the human heart; yet no one can fathom what God has done from beginning to end.

Ecclesiastes 3:11 (NIV)

My father closed the door behind him as he left the rehab. The click of the latch in the jam sounded like death to me, but it was really the sound of my new life beginning. I stood there, completely transfixed for about a minute, staring at the door. I was trying to come to terms with where I was and what was happening, but all I wanted to do was run out the door and find my father.

"Hi, you must be Nina." I was startled when I heard the voice come from behind me, and I turned around to see the source. Standing behind the counter in the lobby was a pretty, middle-aged woman with brown hair. Her sparkling green eyes were gentle and kind, and her soft, slight smile was sympathetic. This was not her first rodeo. I was experiencing a crucial moment in my life, and she fully understood the gravity of the situation.

She did not move around the counter to get closer to me. She just stood there and patiently waited for me to answer.

I tried to muster up a shred of dignity and wiped away the tears from my eyes. I answered, "Yes, I'm Nina." My name was the only thing I was sure of at that moment because I was already questioning my decision to be there.

"It's nice to meet you, Nina. My name is Diane. I'm the nurse here. Why don't you come behind the counter? My office is right here, and I can go over some things with you." I wondered what "things" she was talking about. I didn't like the sound of it already.

Part of me hesitated, but where could I go? I didn't have a car parked outside, my father was gone, and I was an emotional wreck. I had no other options, so I went behind the counter and followed her into her office.

Her office was tiny. At best, it was the size of a large closet. As I sat in the chair by her desk, it felt like the walls were closing in on me. She opened her drawer and took out a blood pressure device. When she started to pull the armband open, and I heard the grating sound of the velcro ripping apart, I started breathing deeply to slow my heartbeat because it felt wild in my chest. Diane waited for me as I inhaled and exhaled deeply, and then I nodded to indicate I was ready. I dreaded hearing what the reading would be because I imagined that it wouldn't be good. I was only sober for a little over a week, but it felt like an eternity to me. I hadn't gone for more than three days without a drink in almost two decades.

My blood pressure was a bit high, but not as bad as I thought it would be. Then Diane said, "I'll need to weigh you now." When I asked why, I didn't hide the anger in my voice. I've always struggled with my weight, so the last thing I wanted to do was get on a scale and feel worse about myself. She said, "I have to keep track of your vitals and weight while you're here to ensure there aren't any issues."

Then Diane asked me how I'd been feeling since I stopped drinking. She wanted to know if I noticed or felt anything unusual. I responded, "Yes, I've had the shakes, and my calves are swollen."

At the mention of my swollen calves, her face took on an entirely different expression; she looked concerned. In a solemn voice, she said, "Let me see them." I pulled up my pant legs and showed her. Immediately, she started touching them and gently squeezed my ankles. I could tell that Diane didn't like what she saw when she said, "I see what you're saying. We will have to keep an eye on that."

Diane also explained that she had to go through my purse because I wasn't allowed access to my cell phone and was only permitted a pack of cigarettes a day. She gave me a few packs from the carton I brought but said I needed to make sure I didn't smoke them too quickly. I scoffed sarcastically in response to her instructions, and she immediately said, "Is that an issue?" I was about to tell her that it was, that I was a grown woman and that it was ridiculous, but I stopped myself. I was too tired to argue, so I just shook my head, "No."

After Diane finished going over everything with me, she said she was bringing me to meet my therapist because he needed to fill out my admission paperwork. As we exited her office, I saw a woman standing in the lobby. Diane introduced us. The woman's name was Melanie; as it turned out, she was the only other person at the rehab. I was shocked to hear that, but not as much as Melanie was. She said she thought I was a new employee, not a client. It was an awkward moment, so I laughed to ease the tension. Then, Diane and I walked down the hall to the therapist's office. When she knocked on the door, I heard a male voice say, "Come in." Diane opened the door, and I saw a man younger than me sitting at a desk. He had a welcoming smile when he asked me to sit down.

To best describe my emotional state, the first time I stepped into the office of Christopher Michael Burns, LCSW, CSAT, I would say that I felt like an abused and wounded animal who had been living on the streets for years. The kind of animal you see in those online videos when people film their attempts at rescue. You always see the animal cowering in fear yet acting out in anger because they try to protect themselves the best way they know how. First, they distance themselves from others, and then they go into attack mode when anyone draws near. They do that because they believe no one can be trusted. They do that because they equate people to pain. When I entered his office, I felt no different than the animals you see in those videos. That's exactly where I was emotionally the first time I met my therapist, Chris Burns. That's how tortured my soul was when I first got to the rehab.

I only vaguely remember Chris introducing himself to me and responding in kind. However, I do recall the paperwork he had to fill out and some that he gave me. Chris handed me a paper with a long list of things you could ask for help with as a patient. If you wanted help with something, you would put a checkmark next to it. I wound up checking off almost everything on that list.

All of my emotional and spiritual battle wounds needed to be healed, and the only way I was going to achieve that was by tending to them. As with all wounds, they will become infected if left unattended for a long time. By the time I got to the rehab, my heart and soul were infected with bitterness, resentment, anger, envy, shame, and sorrow because I had chosen to numb my pain for seventeen years instead of addressing it.

While filling out the required paperwork, I stopped occasionally to look around his office. I was trying to adjust to my surroundings because the situation still felt surreal. Almost as if I were an outsider observing this monumental moment in my life. I saw his degrees as I looked at the office walls, but then I saw a guitar. Seeing it jolted me back to reality. It took me a moment to process what I was looking at, and my next thought was, *Is my new therapist also a musician?* That seemed highly unlikely to me, so I felt compelled to ask, "Do you play guitar?" and he answered very matter-of-factly, "Yes, and I also sing."

Chris immediately returned to filling out the required paperwork for my admission as I sat there, stunned.

I must say that afterward, I felt an overwhelming peace come over me and an inexplicable knowing. My next thought was, *It's going to be okay. I'm going to be okay.*

The peace I felt at that moment came from God. Only He can provide exquisite, divine peace, and that's exactly what I experienced. Also, the certainty I had that all would be well? I know that also came from the Lord. I believe seeing that guitar was supposed to awaken me from my reverie. It brought me back to the land of the living, allowing me to recognize the musical "sign" in front of me. I believe that was God's way of letting me know I was in the right place.

Once Chris completed my paperwork, he turned to me and said, "So, tell me why you're here."

I sighed deeply and replied, "I'm an alcoholic with anger management issues, and pride is my greatest sin."

I remember him pausing at my candid yet succinct confession. Then Chris said, with a wry smile, "So, you know yourself." He seemed a bit shocked at my candor and perhaps with my assessment of myself. I was surprised that I admitted that pride was my greatest sin, not that it wasn't true, but rather that I spoke so honestly about my sin.

There's something freeing about being at the end of your rope because, in a way, you just don't care anymore. You don't care how you appear or what people think. At least, that's what it did for me. It was easy to be brutally honest about my brokenness because I could no longer hide it.

We spoke a little more, and then Chris said that one of their behavioral technicians would take me to the house where I would be staying.

I have to say that I derived more hope and comfort from seeing that guitar than I did any of his degrees on the wall, which is not that far-fetched if you think about it. Music was my refuge and therapy for most of my life until I walked away from it. Singing rescued me emotionally more times than I could count, so understandably, a symbol of my former sanctuary would inspire hope in me.

My many wounds had finally stripped me of my false pride. At last, I was willing to concede that I couldn't figure out my life or addiction on my own. I was surrendering, which is what I needed to do before I could start anew. I had to admit defeat in my long-fought battle against my traumas and addiction; if I ever wanted to declare victory in the war, I was fighting for myself and my life.

I didn't realize it at the time, but this was the exact moment when my flesh started to die, and my spirit began to be revived.

> *For if you live according to the flesh, you will die; but if by the Spirit you put to death the misdeeds of the body, you will live. For those who are led by the Spirit of God are the children of God.*
>
> Romans 8:13-14 (NIV)

My first week at the rehab was incredibly difficult. I craved alcohol to the point that it made me feel like clawing at my own throat. My body was harshly objecting to the imposed withdrawal of the very thing that had been killing it.

My mood swings were intense; one minute, I would be happy that I was sober; the next, frustrated and desperate for a drink, and then bitter about having the disease of addiction and completely ashamed about what my life had become.

I also missed my babies terribly and would frequently have flashbacks about how I left them and where I left them. I would often wonder what became of them, but I would constantly try to push those thoughts out of my mind as quickly as possible because the horrific scenarios I imagined made my heart feel like a vise was gripping it. The guilt, shame, and worry I felt were agonizing and left me in tears.

However, a few motivating factors enabled me to keep pushing forward. The first was my immense desire to stop hating myself and my life, although I was highly doubtful at the time that I would ever feel differently. I had felt that way for so long but was utterly exhausted by my constant inner turmoil, so I was determined to try. I had to. I simply couldn't continue going on the way I had been.

The second was my family. I desperately wanted to repair my ruined relationships and earn back their trust. I dreamt of the day they would look at me again with pride instead of worry and anguish.

The third motivating factor was my babies, Derek and Maxi. They deserved so much more than I was able to give them. I had tried my best to give them a good life while I had them, and I do know that they were happy most of the time, but the way I left them haunted me.

You might think my first reason should have been my family, but let me explain why you'd be wrong. In recovery, we learn very early on that we have to want sobriety for ourselves, first and foremost. Quite often, we are unsuccessful if we pursue it for anyone else. It just doesn't seem to stick. Self-motivation and determination are essential to our recovery because it means we finally believe we deserve a better life.

It didn't take me long to realize that I had to be just as tenacious about staying sober as I was in the past about getting drunk. During my journey in recovery, I have learned how to transfer that intensity into pursuing sobriety. My energy is now directed towards rebuilding myself and my life, where it was once spent destroying both.

During my first week at the rehab, we were told that we had to go to the gym or church on Sundays. Now, to be clear, I hadn't voluntarily stepped foot into a church since my mother, Carmen, had passed. Sure, I'd attended church for weddings and baptisms during those years, but those were obligations. I went to support other people out of respect for their occasions, but I had no desire to be there. However, when asked what I wanted to do on that first Sunday at the rehab, I chose the church because something inside nudged me to go.

I'll never forget the first time I went to Sunday service at theCross. The behavioral technician at the rehab, who was in charge of Melanie and me, drove us in the van to a strip mall. When I saw all the stores, I asked him where we were going because we were supposed to attend church, and he said, "The church is here."

I was flabbergasted. A church in a strip mall? I laughed inwardly at the absurdity of it. I was raised Catholic in New York and was accustomed to churches in a traditional setting. This was a church operating out of a storefront. Who ever heard of such a thing? Needless to say, I was very skeptical. Cynical is also an appropriate word to describe my state of mind because I thought, *There is no way I'm going to get anything out of this. What a waste of time. I should have gone to the gym.*

I stepped out of the van and walked towards the door. As I looked around, all I saw were happy, smiling faces while people chatted outside with one another. A woman was standing by the front door and opened it as she warmly welcomed us to the church.

As I stepped inside, I had every emotional wall erected. I already decided that I wouldn't be moved in any way. I had my mind made up that I would just grin and bear the service. I also made a mental note to tell the technician I wanted to go to the gym the following Sunday.

We sat in the last row, and service started. I waited for the pastor to come out to deliver the sermon, but the service didn't start that way. No, instead, it began with music. The first song was joyous and upbeat, and I swayed slightly to the music. That intrigued me because I had never experienced anything like that in church before. Then, the following two songs were slow, and I felt the beautiful music pierce through my hardened heart. My walls came crumbling down, and I started crying hysterically. I couldn't stop. Tears were streaming down my face because all the pain I felt started seeping out of my soul. I couldn't hold it in anymore. My facade of fierceness melted away, and without even intending to, I found myself surrendering my pain and anguish to the Lord. In those moments, I felt the presence of God so profoundly. I couldn't deny it; what staggered me the most was that I didn't even want to try. I needed God desperately, and for the first time in twenty-seven years since my mother's death, I found myself reaching out to Him.

This was a pivotal moment in my life. It was the day that I met what would become my church family because I had found my church. It was also the day my Lord left the ninety-nine to get me. He welcomed me back with open arms, and I ran to Him with my broken heart.

> *What do you think? If a man owns a hundred sheep, and one of them wanders away, will he not leave the ninety-nine on the hills and go to look for the one that wandered off? And if he finds it, truly I tell you, he is happier about that one sheep than about the ninety-nine that did not wander off.*
>
> Matthew 18:12–13 (NIV)

The beauty of God is infinite because His love is infinite, but what truly amazes me is that He will meet us right where we are. In our brokenness, in the muck and the mire, despite every bad choice we've ever made, all the Lord requires is that you make one good choice. To let Him love you. That's all He wants, but that is everything to God.

God knew exactly how to reach me because He created me. When the Lord knit me together in my mother's womb, He instilled in me an incredible love for music. As a child, my passion for music and singing sustained me, but on that day, God used it to reach me so that He could save me. My Lord and Savior dropped His anchor into my soul and used music as the rope.

> *For you created my inmost being; you knit me together in my mother's womb.*
>
> Psalm 139:13 (NIV)

On that day, I learned that God loves me just as I am at all times. He reached out to me with His unconditional love, and there was no judgment.

That made me realize that the emotional burdens I carried around were my own. That was how I felt about myself and my life. Those horrible feelings had grown from deep within my heart and soul and taken root. They had become permanent residents in the dwelling of my being. I no longer wanted them to reside there and knew they had to be replaced with something else because such spaces never remain empty. What we choose to fill the void with is up to us, and I chose Jesus.

Truer still, He chose me.

There is a song by Elevation Worship called "Graves into Gardens" that I love because it perfectly describes what happened to me that day. God was pulling me out of the grave I dug for myself and was bringing me back into the land of the living. I didn't realize it then, but I was embarking on a journey with the Lord where He would show me that my life could be a beautiful garden again if I only let Him tend to it. My will had made a mess of my life; only God's will would get me out of it. God wanted to do what I couldn't do for myself, and I was finally ready to let Him.

> *He lifted me out of the slimy pit, out of the mud and mire; he set my feet on a rock and gave me a firm place to stand. He put a new song in my mouth, a hymn of*

> *praise to our God. Many will see and fear the Lord and put their trust in him.*
>
> Psalm 40:2-3 (NIV)

During my second week at the rehab, I had to go to the emergency room. The swelling in my calves was getting severe. When the nurse weighed me, she discovered that I had gained seven pounds of water weight. I had been in a constant state of dehydration for many years due to my alcoholism, so unfortunately, my body was stubbornly retaining the fluids that I was consuming. It was extremely painful. It felt like my calves would burst open because my skin was stretched unbelievably tight from the swelling. I had great difficulty walking, so they decided to have one of the technicians take me to the hospital.

When we got there, I went to check in and met the most amazing woman. She asked me why I was there, so I told her about the swelling in my legs and also mentioned that I was in rehab because I was an alcoholic. She couldn't have been more lovely and non-judgmental about my confession. I spoke to her about my struggles, admitting to her that I had planned to kill myself about two weeks prior but that God had stopped me. I remember her eyes looking incredibly sad; it looked like she would cry, but she managed to stop. Afterward, she encouraged me, telling me that she believed I would be successful in my recovery. I couldn't believe I was speaking to her so honestly, but it felt like I'd known her forever. There was an instant comfort and camaraderie that I could not explain. She also went to great lengths to find charitable assistance for the bill I would incur because I had no insurance. She felt like my guardian angel, and I told her as much.

I hadn't gotten her name during our entire time together, so before I left her, I asked what it was. I told her I wanted to thank God for allowing me to meet her because she had taken such good care of me.

I almost fell out of my seat when she told me her name. She pointed at her name tag and said, "My name is Carmen."

Looking down at her name tag in shock, I said, "My mother's name was Carmen."

Then, I looked back up and saw that she was smiling. Instantly, a huge smile spread across my face as well. No words needed to be said because we immediately understood we were destined to meet that day. It wasn't a coincidence; it was a God incident. It's amazing and miraculous how God sends the perfect people to help us on our journeys. Like pieces to a divine puzzle that only He can solve, He puts things together incredibly. Often, we reflect and see His masterpieces in hindsight, but on that day, both I and Carmen were fully aware that ours was not a chance encounter.

When my name finally got called, I was seen by a doctor, and I told him why I was there. He took a look at my legs and was concerned that it might be a heart-related issue. I told him I wanted more than just a chest X-ray. I also wanted bloodwork done to check my kidney and liver function. That was unusual for me because, in active addiction, I always avoided dealing with things that frightened me. However, that day, I wanted to know what I was dealing with. I needed to know what damage I had done to my body, and the doctor agreed.

It took a couple of hours to get the results back, but it felt like days. I kept crying on and off while waiting, and the technician who came with me could not calm me down. I held my breath when the doctor arrived because I anticipated the worst. Then he said, "Your kidney and liver function are within normal limits." I just stared at him because I was convinced there must have been a mistake. The doctor went on to say, "You're okay to go home. I'd rather not prescribe anything for your legs because your body will naturally start eliminating the excess water."

I finally found my voice and said, "Are you sure those are my results? My name is Nina Pajonas. Is that the name you have there?"

The doctor looked at the report and said, "Yes, that's the name I have here. You're good to go."

I started bawling, but they were tears of immense joy and relief. Even the technician started tearing up. As the doctor left the room, I shook my head and said to the technician, "I can't believe it. That is a miracle. It makes no sense that my kidneys and liver are functioning normally. Not with the way I drank."

The technician looked at me and said, "Take the win. Let's get you out here and back to the house."

I was in a state of shock and euphoria as we drove back. I could barely utter a word. Between meeting Carmen and getting such wonderful test results, I was fully confident that the Lord was declaring victory in the war I was fighting for my life.

In the weeks that followed, I would feel moments of indescribable joy and others of overwhelming sorrow. For me, getting sober felt like I was waking up from a coma. I was amongst the living again, and with that came a torrent of emotions. It was exhilarating yet exhausting. All the emotions I had suppressed over the years were rising to the surface, and they all wanted immediate attention. It felt like I was playing emotional Whac-A-Mole because every time I tried to tend to one of my wounds, another memory would pop up to remind me that there was much more work to be done.

Deep introspection after so many years of denial and suppression is not easy. I had to look at all the things that I hadn't wanted to see or acknowledge and dissect them. The close examination was brutal but vital because I had to be honest with myself and my therapist as to what my part was in my demise. In active addiction, we blame everyone and everything else. In sobriety, I had to learn to be accountable for my actions and the consequences that ensued.

I was finally starting to grow up. That might sound peculiar because I was forty-four years old, so let me explain. Emotional immaturity is prevalent in all people with an addiction. We don't emotionally mature past the age we were when we first started abusing substances. So, in my case, I was a twenty-seven-year-old trapped in a forty-four-year-old's body. However, that twenty-seven-year-old had a lot of misguided notions and dysfunctional skill sets that had developed from early childhood, so I had an enormous amount of work cut out for me. It was daunting, but I was determined and fully supported along the way by my therapist and my family.

I started to pray every night before I went to bed. I would talk to God for an hour or more, crying profusely while asking for His forgiveness and the ability to forgive myself.

I wish guilt were the only emotion that tortured my soul because that would have been bearable. However, it wasn't just guilt I felt, but shame. There is a huge and distinct difference. Guilt tells me I've done something wrong, that I've sinned, while shame tells me that the essence of me is wrong, that I am sin.

Shame had kept me in a cycle of sin for so many years. It is the narrative and weapon of the enemy, and he is an expert at using it. He had used shame to defeat and destroy me throughout my life. If I continued to let it live my soul, I would have continued to condemn myself, and there is no condemnation in Christ. I would have declared myself hopeless and would not have turned to our Living Hope.

> *Therefore, since we are surrounded by such a great cloud of witnesses, let us throw off everything that hinders and the sin that so easily entangles. And let us run with perseverance the race marked out for us, fixing our eyes on Jesus, the pioneer and perfecter of faith. For the joy set before him he endured the cross, scorning its shame, and sat down at the right hand of the throne of God.*
>
> Hebrews 12:1-2 (NIV)

I love that passage of scripture for many reasons, but after reading it numerous times, one part in particular stood out to me: Jesus scorned the shame of the cross. I believe such strong verbiage was used intentionally to make it exceedingly clear how He feels about that emotion.

That inspired me to ask myself a crucial question: If our Lord and Savior despised shame in His story, isn't it safe to say He would despise it in the stories of His children? The answer, of course, is *yes*. That is when I realized I had to learn to scorn shame if I was ever going to fulfill God's plans and purpose for my life, which was the joy set out before me.

> *As Scripture says, "Anyone who believes in him will never be put to shame."*
>
> Romans 10:11 (NIV)

Unfortunately, I was still struggling with my mental obsession with alcohol. Every day when I woke up, it was the first thing on my mind, and immediately, my body would react by responding with an intense physical craving that made me want to crawl out of my skin. Every night, when I prayed, I begged the Lord to take the obsession away from me because it made me weary.

About three weeks into my stay at the rehab, I woke up one morning and went into the kitchen to make myself a cup of coffee. I was awake for nearly an hour when it hit me: I hadn't thought of alcohol at all. I had gotten up like a normal human being with nothing else on my mind but starting my day. Joy surged like a tidal wave in my soul at that realization. God had relieved me of my mental obsession just as I asked Him to! He had answered my urgent prayer yet again.

Jesus is also referred to as The Great Physician, so I have no doubt in my mind that He alone granted me freedom from the chains of addiction that bound me. I don't know when the Lord began healing me, but the first evidence of it was in the hospital when I received the unbelievable test results from my blood work that my liver and kidneys were functioning normally. Then, He relieved me of the mental obsession and the physical compulsion that I had been suffering from for nearly two decades. My Lord and Savior is loving but also merciful. He heard my weary cries for help and showed me compassion. I know alcoholics in recovery who have far more years of sobriety than I do, and they still struggle with those things, so I know I'm exceedingly blessed that I no longer suffer those burdens.

I will always be in awe of God's greatness and goodness, just as I will always marvel at His ability to take our mistakes and turn them into miracles.

> *And the prayer offered in faith will make the sick person well; the Lord will raise them up. If they have sinned, they will be forgiven.*
>
> James 5:15

While I was at the rehab, my therapist, Chris, gave me multiple assignments to work on as part of my therapy. However, there was a specific project he tasked me with that meant the most to me personally. Chris asked me to create a body map, which is essentially a drawing showing how I felt in active addiction.

In the picture I drew, I was almost completely submerged in a body of water that I called the Sea of Sorrow. I had also drawn a chain that wrapped around my ankle, and at the end of it, there was an anchor.

When I discussed the picture with Chris, I told him that the anchor represented my addiction because that's what it felt like when I was drinking. My alcoholism would weigh me down, pulling me under the water and deeper into the Sea of Sorrow. Then, I would swim back up to the surface to catch my breath, but inevitably, it would pull me under again. I was proud of the picture because it perfectly represented how I had felt and how I never wanted to feel again.

During my recovery, I have gone from drowning in the Sea of Sorrow to swimming in the Sea of Salvation. However, I take no credit for such a tremendous transition and transformation. I have my Lord and Savior, Jesus Christ, to thank for that. His love and mercy for my soul took me out of one and delivered me to the other.

> *But I pray to you, Lord, in the time of your favor; in your great love, O God, answer me with your sure salvation. Do not let the floodwaters engulf me or the depths swallow me up or the pit close its mouth over me. Answer me, Lord, out of the goodness of your love; in your great mercy turn to me.*
>
> James 69:13, 15-16 (NIV)

Things had been progressing well for me at the rehab, but unfortunately, on Christmas day, I had a setback. I didn't relapse, thank God, but I acted out in a major way. It was just as much a surprise to me as it was to everyone else who witnessed or heard about it, but unfortunately, it happened.

Initially, the owner of the rehab told Melanie and me that we would attend one twelve-step meeting and go to the movies on Christmas. That had been the plan for about two weeks. However, on Christmas Day, she changed her mind. She decided we would go to two meetings instead of one.

No one but God Himself could have predicted my gross overreaction to an additional meeting. I didn't even understand the surge of anger that I immediately felt when she altered the plans. I was livid! I felt my blood pressure rising, and I started yelling and cursing. I didn't do it while the owner was there; I exploded after she left. Unfortunately, it was also ongoing.

A little while later, Melanie, the technician on duty, and I went to the movie theater. I was muttering angrily under my breath the entire way there. Once we arrived, I left the van quickly and walked off to have a cigarette by myself. I started staring at a small trash can as I stood there smoking. Then, I suddenly thought, *I'm going to kick this thing clear across the parking lot!* So, I drew back my leg and swung it forward hard and fast. Then, just as my foot was about to connect with the trash can, I slowed my leg abruptly. I wound up only tapping the trash can, which made it wobble slightly, but it stayed upright. It was pretty anti-climatic, to say the least!

After my major display of immaturity, I stormed inside the theater while the technician looked on in confusion. Once the movie ended, he drove us to the second meeting we were supposed to attend, and afterward, we all returned to the house. I was in a horrible mood throughout the entire day, and I struggled to understand why I felt so angry.

Being that it was a holiday, my therapist, Chris, held a session with me when he returned to work to discuss what happened. The look on his face when I walked into his office saddened me because it was evident that he was disappointed in me. Once I sat down, he asked me what happened, so I told him everything. Then Chris asked me why I got so angry by a simple change in the schedule, and I responded that I didn't want to go to an additional meeting because I wanted more of the day to relax. I also told him I was sad about not spending the holiday with my family and missed my baby boys. All of which was true. However, none of those things were the real reason for my anger, and Chris quickly told me that. I got mad at him because I felt he was calling me a liar, but he wasn't. Chris was simply pushing me to find my truth. He wasn't going to let me lie to myself, even unintentionally.

Finally, I blurted out, "Who does she think she is? Nobody tells me what to do! Nobody controls me!"

Then, Chris tapped his nose and said, "Bingo, there we have it. That's the reason."

I must say that I was very annoyed when he said that, but he was right. Yes, I was upset about those other things, but they weren't the motivating factors for my temper tantrum. It's embarrassing to admit, but it was a tantrum. I acted like a child. That was my setback.

I even tried joking with Chris, saying, "At least I didn't kick it across the parking lot! I wanted to, and old Nina would have! Don't the twelve-step programs say, 'Progress, not perfection?'"

Chris gave me a look that told me he didn't appreciate my joke. He told me that I could have been kicked out of the rehab because of my behavior. I was stunned when he said that. During my entire meltdown, I never imagined that could be a consequence of my actions.

I will say that I learned a very valuable lesson that day. My therapist, Chris, taught me that I had to be honest with myself and others at all times. He showed me how to dig deep within to get to the truth so that I could address the root cause of unwanted and undesirable behavior. It was a vital lesson, and as embarrassing as the situation was, I'm glad I learned it with him at the rehab. Had it not happened while I was there, that setback might have led to a relapse.

I also learned that a bad day can be beneficial if I learn from it. When I'm triggered emotionally, I have an opportunity to learn even more about myself, which allows me to grow further, both in my sobriety and spirituality.

> *You used to walk in these ways, in the life you once lived. But now you must also rid yourselves of all such things as these: anger, rage, malice, slander, and filthy language from your lips. Do not lie to each other, since*

> *you have taken off your old self with its practices and have put on the new self, which is being renewed in knowledge in the image of its Creator.*
>
> Colossians 3:7-10 (NIV)

On December 31, 2017, I got baptized at my church, theCross. Earlier that month, the church had announced that they would be doing baptisms, and I felt strongly that it was something I needed to do to honor my renewed relationship with the Lord. I had been baptized as an infant, but obviously, my parents made that decision for me. Though I must say, I'm pleased that they did. However, my commitment to Christ was now my choice, as was my new life of recovery. In my mind, heart, and soul, both things needed to be celebrated and boldly marked by baptism because it represented the new creation I was becoming.

It was such a beautiful day. I was one of many people who waited in line to be baptized, and I was extremely nervous. When they called my name, I walked up to our founding and lead pastor, Zach Zehnder. He smiled at me as he helped me step into the tub of water. Then he spoke the words of baptism over me as I leaned my head back to be submerged. As I came back up and out of the water, I felt exhilarated because I had officially turned my life over to Jesus. Then Pastor Zach helped me step out of the tub, and I started walking up the aisle. I only took a few steps when I heard my friends call out my name excitedly, which made me smile.

Between my time at the rehab and the church, I quickly made new friends. Some were in recovery, like myself, and some were just lovely people I met while attending Sunday services. It was such a wonderful way to start my new life, and I treasure all the people who have been with me since the beginning of my journey.

When it was all said and done, I wound up spending Thanksgiving, Christmas, and New Year in rehab. My last day at the rehab was January 4, 2018. It was also my mother Carmen's birthday; she would have been seventy-one years old. My mother died when she was forty-four years old, and I got sober at forty-four years old. She went home to be with the Lord, and the Lord saved my life at the very same age. So, I ask, was that yet another coincidence? I think not. I believe it was part of His carefully designed and divine plan. The Lord works in very mysterious ways.

I was overjoyed to be released on my mother's birthday! I received it as confirmation that my journey was blessed and that God and my mother were watching over me.

> *It has seemed good to me to show the signs and wonders that the Most High God has done for me.*
>
> Daniel 4:2 (ESV)

After being in rehab, going back home filled me with anxiety. Returning to the real world after living in such a controlled environment is very intimidating. My first order of business was getting to a twelve-step meeting right after I got home. My therapist, Chris, stressed that I should get to one on the same day because I was being released early in the day. I also had to be back at the rehab the next day to start my outpatient treatment.

Before I left the rehab, Chris gave me a list of twelve-step meetings in my town that I could go to. As I started to review the list, I realized that I didn't need it, and I told him so. Immediately afterward, I saw a shocked and worried look on his face, so I quickly reminded him of the two months of sobriety I had achieved a couple of years prior.

Chris looked relieved and happy when I said that I used to attend the same meeting consistently back then and that I would do so again.

When I got home later that day, I was only in my parent's house for about an hour before I left to go to the meeting. However, once I got there, I sat outside. The meeting hadn't started yet, so I knew I wasn't late, but I couldn't bring myself to go inside. I was worried that the people in the group would remember me and judge me. Then I worried that they wouldn't remember me and that I would feel hurt. I sat there for several minutes, flooded with fear, until the door opened, and I saw an older man with gray hair and kind blue eyes. He looked at me with a big smile on his face and said, "I remember you! What are you doing out here? Come inside!"

Instantly, my anxiety turned into relief as I followed the man inside. As he walked me over to the coffee station, he said, "I'm Daniel."

Immediately, I smiled and said, "I'm Nina." Then, as I poured a cup of coffee and prepared it, I told him, "I stopped coming because I started drinking again. I just got out of rehab today. I was sitting outside because I was too embarrassed to come in. I'm so glad you opened the door."

Daniel smiled warmly at me again and said, "I'm glad you came back."

As I sat in the meeting that night, I reflected on the last time I was there. Two years prior, I knew I needed to be there, but I didn't want to be. I tried to convince myself that I wasn't as sick as the rest of the people in the room, but I was lying to myself.

Everyone in the fellowship, that's what we call it, has the disease of addiction. Some of us have multiple addictions, while some only have one, but it doesn't matter one way or the other. The only thing that does matter is that we learn from one another and are there to support each other on our journeys.

As iron sharpens iron, so one person sharpens another.

Proverbs 27:17 (NIV)

It felt like someone had pushed the fast-forward button on my life after over a month of moving in slow motion. It was overwhelming trying to keep up with the new pace. I was also trying my best to settle back in with my parents while settling into my new life. It was quite the juggling act. However, all in all, things were going very well. I was re-establishing my relationship with my parents, myself, and God. Thankfully, I developed a healthy routine that enabled me to be quite productive. I attended my outpatient sessions Monday through Friday and would go to a twelve-step meeting every day. Then, I would drive to my church on Sundays to attend service.

Sunday was always my favorite day because I loved hearing the sermons and learning more about the gospel. I listened very carefully to the lessons our lead pastor, Zach Zehnder, was preaching and tried to implement them in my life because I wanted to walk faithfully with the Lord. To build a new life, I had to do new things. And to be a better person, I needed to grow. I believed then, as I do now, that my life of sobriety had to be built on a foundation of faith. If Christ was the rock on which I stood, I would be secure. I needed more of Him and less of me, and that remains true today.

He must become greater; I must become less.

John 3:30 (NIV)

During my fourth month of recovery, I started to wrestle with survivor's guilt. I simply couldn't understand why God had saved my life when so many other people die from the disease of addiction.

I truly believed I wasn't worth saving. I wasn't a wife or mother and thought that meant my life wasn't as valuable. Throughout my life, I always felt inferior because I hadn't achieved those things. I felt irrelevant, and I thought that God should feel the same way about me.

I found myself crying often over what seemed like the futility of my existence. I questioned the Lord's judgment because I couldn't comprehend why He saved a forty-four-year-old, single, alcoholic woman who had led a very unremarkable life.

I was chasing after God's heart, but I couldn't understand why He was chasing after mine.

I hadn't been sober long, yet I already knew that everything I had tried to do with my life prior had been pointless. Living in my own will all those years had left me completely unfulfilled.

Ultimately, it did not and could not satisfy my soul because I wasn't serving God's intended purpose for my life, and His purpose and plan supersedes all others.

> *Many are the plans in a person's heart, but it is the Lord's purpose that prevails.*
>
> Proverbs 19:21 (NIV)

My spiritual struggle lasted for weeks until I experienced a breakthrough that I'll never forget. It happened on a Sunday at about four o'clock in the morning. I woke up from a sound sleep and immediately started crying. I felt overwhelmed by confusion and sorrow because I didn't know what to do with my life. Simply being sober and remaining sober didn't feel like enough. I wanted to do more. I wanted to be more.

I climbed out of bed with a great sense of urgency. Then, without even thinking about it, I reverted to my childhood habit of kneeling on the floor and crossing my hands in prayer. Tears were still streaming down my face as I prayed for God to show me what my purpose was.

I also told the Lord how grateful I was that He saved me and that I wanted to dedicate my life to Him. I begged my creator to give my life meaning. I asked God to mold me into what He imagined me to be before the beginning of time.

I prayed for a long time, pouring my heart out to the Lord like I used to at the rehab. Once I was done, I climbed back into bed and quickly fell back asleep.

> *I cry out to God Most High, to God who fulfills his purpose for me.*
>
> Psalm 57:2 (ESV)

A couple of hours later, my alarm went off, and I woke up again. I started getting ready for church, but my mood was entirely different. I wasn't sad anymore. I was excited.

When I got to church, I sat in my usual seat and waited for the service to begin. Every Sunday, the beginning of the service consists of worship and the morning announcements. It was during those announcements that God delivered an answer to my prayers.

Pastor Jacob Baumann started speaking to the congregation about the next steps they could take with the church, and as soon as he said those words, I started listening intently. He said that serving others was our next step as children of Christ, but also mentioned that we had to take a series of classes, given by the church, before doing so.

After the service ended, I found Pastor Jacob and told him that I prayed to God that morning because I wanted to know what His plan and purpose were for my life. I also asked when the next class was and signed up for it immediately.

The Lord spoke to me through Pastor Jacob that day; I know He did. My Savior gave me the direction I needed and longed for. After I completed the classes, I started serving in the children's ministry. When I think about it now, I realize just how fitting that was. As the children were getting to know God, I was re-establishing my relationship with Him. As they learned scripture for the first time, I was rediscovering it. It was a very significant time for all of us because we were taking baby steps in faith together.

I know that the Lord wanted me to take care of His children, but I also believe He wanted me to learn from them. A child's faith is so pure; it is so absolute. It is one of the most beautiful things to witness because it is spotless and steadfast. I believe with all my heart and soul that the Lord wanted me to adopt the faith of a child. Their innocence creates a fullness of faith that far exceeds their size, and He wanted the same for me. That's why God put me there.

Slowly, surely, and steadily, my Heavenly Father was establishing a strong foundation for my faith and future calling.

> *Truly I tell you, anyone who will not receive the kingdom of God like a little child will never enter it.*
>
> Mark 10:15 (NIV)

When I was six months sober, my world was turned upside down when we discovered that my stepmother, Evelyn, had breast cancer. As soon as I heard the news, I was devastated. It felt like I was reliving the nightmare of my youth when I found out that my biological mother, Carmen, had breast cancer.

After I found out, I sat in my car and cried. I had flashbacks of losing my mother, Carmen. My mind automatically went to the worst-case scenario, which is another common trait among people with an addiction. I started praying to God and expressed my anger and disbelief that this was happening again. "Both mothers, God? One wasn't enough?" I could feel the bitterness and rage starting to build, and instantly, I started craving a drink. I hadn't since rehab, so the feeling startled me because it felt somewhat foreign. Then, I was terrified. All I kept thinking was, *No! I don't want that life anymore. I don't want to be that person again!* I was shaking because my body and mind told me I didn't have to feel those feelings, that there was an escape. The addict in me thought, *I have the right to drink over this!* However, the faithful child of God that I was diligently working to become thought, *This isn't about you. It's about your stepmother who has loved and cared for you almost your entire life.*

I had a choice that day. I could drink and go back to being selfish and self-centered, or I could show up for my mother and father in a way that I was never able to before. I could show true gratitude for all they had done for me. I could be a blessing rather than a burden. Praise be to God; I chose the former and not the latter.

Thankfully, I also had my fellowship to lean on. About ten minutes after I had the thought of drinking, I headed to a meeting. I got to the clubhouse and admitted to everyone there that I was struggling and why. When we huddled in a circle at the end of the meeting, they all prayed for my mother. Afterward, people came up to hug me and let me cry on them. They gave me their phone numbers, and they told me to call them if I thought of drinking again.

To this day, I have a very special spot in my heart for those who rallied around me in my time of great need and distress. I'll never forget that they supported me when I needed it most. They helped me stay sober another day, and when I woke up the next morning, I was ecstatic that I didn't drink. It solidified my belief that I could handle adversity in sobriety. I learned that new wounds didn't have to destroy me, which was an incredible discovery.

On that day, and in the days that followed, I started to process pain in a more mature and healthy way. I didn't choose to self-sabotage; instead, I chose self-care. What a world of difference it made when I finally came to believe I was worthy of saving instead of destroying. That shift in thought and perception was directly correlated to my walk with Christ. His love taught me how to love myself again. That gave me a true sense of value because His love is firmly rooted in who I am, not in anything I've ever done or will ever do. What a relief that was and still is. After a lifetime of trying desperately to please everyone so that they would like or love me, I finally came to understand that I am divinely loved by my creator simply because I am His child.

It was His love and that of my parents that allowed me to choose life rather than death that day. That might seem like an overly dramatic statement, but I assure you, it is not. I'm an alcoholic. For me, to drink is to die. Perhaps not immediately, but eventually, it would come to that again. However, I can not take credit for the strength it took to make that decision. It was the power of the Holy Spirit at work. It had started removing the toxicity in me and was renewing my heart and soul.

> *In the same way, the Spirit helps us in our weakness. We do not know what we ought to pray for, but the Spirit himself intercedes for us through wordless groans. And he who searches our hearts knows the mind of the Spirit, because the Spirit intercedes for God's people in accordance with the will of God.*
>
> Romans 8:26-27 (NIV)

My stepmother, Evelyn, had a long road ahead, but ultimately she won the battle. I was in awe of the way she handled the diagnosis she received. She never indulged in self-pity, not even briefly. Instead, she wanted to know what her options were so that she could start battling the disease. I was proud of her poise, dignity, and grace throughout the ordeal. I've always respected my stepmother Evelyn tremendously, but my respect for her grew even more during that time. Watching her face adversity of that kind with such immense strength was inspiring. I've been exceedingly blessed to have her in my life since childhood because she is an incredible role model of womanhood. Praise God, she is in remission now, and there has been no trace of cancer in her since.

> *She is clothed with strength and dignity; she can laugh at the days to come. She speaks with wisdom, and*

> *faithful instruction is on her tongue. She watches over the affairs of her household and does not eat the bread of idleness. Her children arise and call her blessed; her husband also, and he praises her: "Many women do noble things, but you surpass them all."*
>
> Proverbs 31:25-29 (NIV)

During that time, I decided that I needed to know what happened to my baby boys. I knew it wasn't the best time to do it because of all that was happening at home, but I couldn't wait any longer. I also knew the likelihood was that they had been put down, but I needed to know for sure. However, I did hope that they were still at the shelter or that they got adopted.

In sobriety, truth is paramount to me, not just with others but with myself. I no longer try to delude myself like I used to. In the past, I avoided things that made me uneasy, and when I couldn't avoid them anymore, I tried to escape, but the escape was merely an illusion. By delaying the inevitable, I only prolonged the pain and compounded it because bad situations never get better with denial; they only get worse. Today, I try my best to tackle things head-on because I no longer want to be controlled by fear.

Let me be clear: my courage comes from Christ. I can only face the present and have faith in the future because He is with me every step of the way.

I looked up the Humane Society website, where I left my boys, to get their address. Then, I called my friend Alicia. When Alicia answered, I asked if she would go to the shelter to find out what became of them. At first, she advised me not to find out. She said, "Ignorance, in this case, is bliss, Nee. I'm worried that if you find out they are gone, it will jeopardize your sobriety."

I paused momentarily and then told her, "It won't. I promise you it won't. What will jeopardize my sobriety is not knowing. I have no closure. I'm living in an emotional limbo because I don't know what happened to my babies."

Alicia sighed deeply and said, "All right, I'll go." I warned her that they might give her a hard time about releasing the information to her, and she replied, "How long have you known me, Nee? I'll find out. You're my girl. I won't leave there until they tell me what happened to your babies." I thanked her profusely, and Alicia told me she would go the next day.

I didn't doubt for one minute that Alicia would find out because she's tenacious, like me. Alicia is a formidable woman, so I knew the people who worked there didn't stand a chance; she would get her way.

When she called me the next day, I let the phone ring a few times before I answered because I knew what I was about to hear would probably break my heart. When I finally picked up the phone and heard her say my name, I knew.

I interrupted her and said, "They're gone, right?"

She said, "Yes."

Then, I cried. Alicia just listened and didn't say a word until I stopped. Then she told me they had been put down the day I left them there. I got so angry when she told me, but she said, "It's better that it happened that way. Imagine how much worse it would have been for them to wait for their mommy, who wasn't coming back. They are with God. He took them home quickly so they wouldn't have to suffer. You should be grateful."

It took me a while, but I eventually calmed down because I realized she was right. It would have been worse for them to have stayed there and waited for me. Of course, I wish I had gotten the chance to save them, to go back for them, but that's not how things happened. I had to accept what was, even though it was not what I wanted it to be.

Acknowledging and accepting the consequences of my actions didn't make my pain go away; it exacerbated it. However, it did mark the beginning of my healing because I could finally grieve the decision I made that day and their deaths. To this day, I still mourn the deaths of my boys, and I know in my heart that I always will.

The reality is that being sober doesn't make life easy, and neither does being a Christian. If I allowed myself to believe that either would make my life a cakewalk, I would be sorely disappointed. However, I do know that being a sober Christian enables me to handle things better because I'm much more mature mentally, emotionally, and spiritually. Therein lies the beauty, even in tragedy. God graciously gives me His strength to deal with situations that normally would have destroyed and defeated me.

I can do all this through him who gives me strength.

Philippians 4:13 (NIV)

Four months later, my therapist, Chris Burns, told me I was ready to fly solo. He said that I didn't need him anymore, and he was right, but unfortunately, it didn't elicit a great response from me because I wasn't ready to hear it.

Chris was my therapist and guide through the most confusing, painful, yet beautiful time in my life. There is so much beauty in a life of recovery, but it's not for the faint of heart. Getting sober is very difficult, but staying sober also has its challenges, and he had seen me through both.

When Chris first met me, I was a broken, bitter, angry, and depressed alcoholic child masquerading as a woman. I had no healthy coping tools, only crutches, and I knew nothing about boundaries. I also had no real sense of self-worth or confidence. What I did have was a lifetime of unhealed traumas that had been eating away at my heart and soul. That's the person Chris met that fateful day in November 2017. That's the condition I was in.

However, it was ten months later, and I had come a long way. I only wish I had enough emotional maturity to handle the situation in a dignified manner, but I didn't. Instead, I got irate when he suggested that we start figuring out when my last session would be. Unfortunately, I have a bad habit of quickly going from sadness to anger when something upsets me. I'm much better at controlling that unhealthy shift now, but at ten months sober, I wasn't able to. Not quite yet, anyway.

When Chris mentioned a final session, I started crying immediately; tears streamed down my face, and they wouldn't stop. Then he asked, "Nina, why are you crying?" He wanted me to express my emotions, but I couldn't. I started speaking but stopped because I didn't want to say what I felt. I had a torrent of emotions bursting out of me, but instead of doing so verbally, they just kept cascading down my face in a river of tears.

I wanted to say, "You're leaving me too? How can you do this to me? I can't do this alone!" But that wasn't true. Chris had taught me that just because you feel something doesn't mean it's accurate. It can be, but it's not a guarantee. Perception is key, and mine was skewed.

Six-year-old Nina might as well have been sitting on that couch in front of him because my abandonment issues were triggered and would soon be on full display. All my sorrow from past disappointments rose to the surface, and I became furious. Then, all of a sudden, I had words, too many words, and they were not-so-nice. I'm embarrassed to admit that I started cursing and raising my voice.

Chris, ever the professional, just sat quietly and let me vent. Thankfully, I eventually ran out of steam. After I did, he explained why I was ready to strike out on my own. I believe that in his delicate way, Chris was trying to tell me I was using him as a crutch, and he was right. Like a child who doesn't feel secure without their favorite blanket, I derived comfort from my therapy sessions with him. However, to have true confidence in my sobriety, it would have to be without him in the equation. As a therapist, Chris knew that, and later, when I was ready to be honest with myself, I knew it too.

It's important to understand that certain things can trigger trauma victims. Similar circumstances, people, or places can bring forth a negative reaction. People in recovery have to deal with this, hence why most twelve-step programs will tell us to avoid people, places, and things that we associate with during our active addiction. They want us to steer clear of triggers that could cause us to relapse. We can't live in a bubble, so it is impossible to prevent every such occurrence, but as people in recovery, we try our best to.

During that session with Chris, my abandonment issue was brought to the surface. I was still young in recovery, so I wasn't yet adept at controlling my reactions to what I perceived were negative situations. However, there was absolutely nothing negative about my situation with Chris. It was actually very positive because he was saying that I was strong enough in my sobriety to stand on my own two feet. I received that message as painful because I felt like he was leaving me, but Chris was saying that I was ready to leave him.

Thankfully, today, I'm much better at dealing with difficult situations, regulating my responses, and pausing to reflect on what I will say before I say it. I don't claim to be perfect at it, but I'm much better than I was. However, at that time, I only had ten months of sobriety under my belt, and now I have over six years. I've made far more progress in those areas because I've had much more practice.

Unfortunately for Chris, I couldn't control or restrain my emotions that day. Although, I did apologize to him almost immediately for my extremely immature behavior. That is something else they teach us in the twelve-step programs. If I have acted inappropriately, inadvertently, or otherwise, I'm supposed to make amends as quickly as possible. The ideal result in any situation is that I've handled it respectfully and maturely; however, if I haven't, I need to hold myself accountable and reflect on how I can handle it better in the future.

My emotional, mental, and spiritual growth requires a commitment to change negative behaviors and responses and replace them with positive ones. That type of dedication is required of people in recovery every day so that we don't fall back into our old destructive patterns and relapse. There is an immense amount of self-reflection and correction that is necessary on my journey of recovery. However, the same can be said of my walk with Christ as a Christian woman. Both require a great deal of work on myself, but my life today is so incredibly joyful and fulfilling that it's worth all the effort.

> *Let perseverance finish its work so that you may be mature and complete, not lacking anything.*
>
> James 1:4 (NIV)

During my first year of recovery, I also had to work on rebuilding the relationships within my family that I had damaged during my active addiction. It takes time to earn back trust, but I did it one day at a time. For my family, a living amends was the only way I could earn their trust back and keep it. A living amends means that I remain focused on my recovery and growth, taking care not to backslide into old attitudes and behaviors.

As I said before, getting sober is very difficult, but staying sober is also challenging. The consistency that is required in recovery involves great discipline. Also, the longer I'm sober, the easier it is to forget just how bad things were when I wasn't. In twelve-step meetings, we always say that the newest person in the room is the most important because they remind us of what it was like when we first started our recovery journeys. They also make us reflect on the end of our active addiction, what got us there, how horrible we felt, and all that we lost along the way. All of which remind us of the greatest gift we have ever received, the one that allowed us to get sober. It's called the gift of desperation, or if you like acronyms, G.O.D, which is quite fitting when you think about it.

During my first year of sobriety, I also worked with many newcomers, specifically women. It is strongly suggested that if we sponsor someone or are sponsored by someone, they be the same gender. Too often, people get into romantic relationships early in recovery, which is dangerous because it can put us in danger of relapsing. The focus needs to be on ourselves so that we can fully develop our new identity while establishing our new life.

My first sponsor was an older woman who was like a mother to me. I adored her and still do. She suggested that I refrain from having any romantic relationships until I was at least a year sober, to which I replied, while laughing, "I can do that standing on my head." The look of shock on her face was comical, but then I went on to explain that I hadn't been with a man since my last boyfriend, the one who almost killed me. She was despondent when I told her what happened but said she was glad I wouldn't be distracted by men.

My sponsor got me deeply involved in the fellowship very quickly. She had me chairing meetings, making coffee, and also brought me to group events centered around recovery. She was amazing; I learned so much from her. To best explain what a sponsor is, I would say that they are mentors. They help us on our journeys by supporting us when we're struggling and teaching us things they've learned.

It struck me as odd at the time, but throughout my first year of sobriety, the men in my recovery home group would have new women sit with me. I was confused by it at first because I was only a few months sober when it started, and there were lots of other women in the room with far more time in recovery than me. However, despite not feeling qualified, I went along with it. It's all about helping the next person in need, and I was happy to do so.

Eventually, I also realized I had more time to do it; I wasn't married and had no children, so I didn't have to rush home after meetings. I had the time and energy necessary to spend with those women.

Then, I had an epiphany: God was using me. Whenever any of the newcomers asked why or how I was so joyful, I told them about my Lord and Savior, Jesus Christ. I would explain how He saved me and all He had done for me. I was spreading the gospel to others in recovery, and it felt as natural as breathing to me.

> *Though you have not seen him, you love him; and even though you do not see him now, you believe in him and are filled with an inexpressible and glorious joy, for you are receiving the end result of your faith, the salvation of your souls.*
>
> 1 Peter 1:8-9 (NIV)

I celebrated my first year in recovery on November 16, 2018. In twelve-step programs, we get a medallion to mark our sobriety anniversaries, and I asked my father, Richard, to give me mine.

My father, usually a very self-controlled man, was highly emotional that night. As he held my medallion in his hand, my father spoke of his pride in my recovery, as well as our family's, until he got so choked up that he could no longer speak. Then, with tears in his eyes, he handed my medallion to me. I cried as I held the coin in the palm of my hand. I watched my father as he walked back to the seat he had been sitting in during the meeting. I couldn't help but think of another time I watched him walk away from me, my first day at the rehab. A year prior, my father was desperately trying to save my life, and now he was celebrating one of the most incredible years of my life.

My biological sister Lisa was also there. She cried as she watched one of the most beautiful and significant moments my father and I have ever shared.

Unfortunately, my stepmother, Evelyn, could not be there due to her cancer treatments. She was advised not to spend time in large groups because her immunity was compromised. My stepsister Lisa and stepbrother John also couldn't be there because neither of them lived in Florida. However, I knew that when my father spoke, he spoke for all of them.

My family supports me incredibly in my recovery. They understand what I need to do to remain sober because I've taught them everything I've learned about my disease. My family has walked this journey with me, offering forgiveness and grace for my past behaviors while sharing in my hope and faith for the future. They have been nothing short of amazing.

Today, I'm completely secure in their love, but with others, there is still a measure of uncertainty in the background. Like the low hum of white noise, my emotional scars whisper to me that I'm unloveable, that I'm never enough of what people want and too much of what they don't want. However, I've learned how to silence that destructive dialogue because I can honestly say I love myself. I praise my Lord and Savior, Jesus Christ, for that because His love taught me how to. God is love, so who can better teach me what it is, what it feels like, and what it can do?

> *Love is patient, love is kind. It does not envy, it does not boast, it is not proud. It does not dishonor others, it is not self-seeking, it is not easily angered, it keeps no record of wrongs. Love does not delight in evil but rejoices with the truth. It always protects, always trusts, always hopes, always perseveres. And now these three remain: faith, hope and love. But the greatest of these is love.*
>
> 1 Corinithians 13:4-7 (NIV)

Shortly after I celebrated my first year of recovery, I auditioned for the worship team at my church. As I mentioned earlier in my story, before my mother Carmen died, she made me promise to continue singing. She had also told me in no uncertain terms that I needed to keep that promise.

So, I couldn't help but think about my mother as I sat in my car before going into the church to audition. I was feeling so many things: anxiety, responsibility, and overwhelming nostalgia. I was very pensive. I even debated not going through with it. Anxiety had my heart beating like a jackrabbit; I felt paralyzed by fear. I couldn't move for several minutes, so I just sat there, lost in my thoughts and memories.

When I sang with bands in bars when I was younger, I knew I wasn't fulfilling my promise to my mother, which bothered me immensely. There had been a burden on my soul for twenty-eight years because no matter how hard I tried, I couldn't figure out how to keep my promise to her.

Amazingly enough, when I finally figured out how to keep that promise, it happened in a very unexpected way. As I mentioned earlier, I had to take a series of classes before I could serve at my church. However, what I didn't mention was the spiritual gift test they had us take at the end of them. When I got my results, it listed several things, but the one that stood out the most was worship. As soon as I read that, I realized what my mother would have wanted me to do. My mother was a great woman of God with enormous faith; she would have wanted me to worship and praise Him through song!

From that day on, I started practicing. I sang worship music every chance I got. Often, I would drive around aimlessly in my car while practicing because I love to sing while I'm driving. I felt immensely passionate about singing again when I hadn't in a very long time. I longed to sing of God's greatness and goodness in the church I had come to love. I wanted to tell the musical story of what He had done in me and my life. I wanted to praise and glorify the Lord with the gift He so graciously gave me.

Finally, I got out of my car and walked across the parking lot. You would think I was going to my execution with how slow I was walking. So many questions were going through my head. What if I froze? What if I wasn't good enough? When I went to audition, I hadn't sung in public for seven years, but I knew I was ready. That's what enabled me to go inside the church that night. I reminded myself that I'd been practicing my singing diligently, preparing for this moment.

I walked in and looked around. I saw some people on the stage, the band members, specifically. Then, our worship director, Kharl Kapp, walked up to me, and I told him I was there to audition. He smiled at me warmly and said he would get Linda, who was in charge of the vocalists. Linda was married to Pastor Mark Crossman, one of three pastors we had at the church. It made me even more nervous to sing in front of the Pastor's wife, but I soon discovered that I had nothing to fear because she was very kind to me.

As I stood there waiting for them, my legs started shaking. Unfortunately, that has happened to me since childhood; whenever I get nervous before singing, my legs shake. It's embarrassing because it's quite visible. I was extremely frustrated by it and tried to calm myself down, but I couldn't.

Soon after, they came back and invited me to sit down. Neither of them could have possibly known how relieved I was to sit. By that point, my legs felt like they were going to crumble beneath me. That's how bad my anxiety was.

Another man came to audition as well, and he sang first. After he did, it was my turn, so I stood up to sing. I sang "Love Like This" by Lauren Daigle. I love that song. The chorus is my favorite part because it's so powerful; "What have I done to deserve love like this? I cannot earn what you so freely give. What have I done to deserve love like this?" I chose that song because that's exactly how I felt about God's love, and I still do.

Once I finished singing, they said I could join the worship team, and I was thrilled! The Lord was putting the pieces of my life and myself back together in the most amazing way.

After I hugged them goodbye, I walked out of the church with childlike excitement. I was overwhelmed by all of my emotions! I was experiencing a mixture of joy, relief, fulfillment, and gratitude. As I walked to my car, I felt lighter, like I was floating on air, which was vastly different from the way I walked in. I felt that way because a burden had been lifted from my soul. I visualized my mother, Carmen, smiling down on me from heaven, and I finally found peace with my promise to her.

I officially started singing with the worship team in January 2019. I remember the first time I saw my name on the schedule to sing on a Sunday; I was so excited! My family was also thrilled because my recovery was bringing back to life the parts of me that had died during my active addiction. My love for singing blossomed again, but so did my love for writing and, unfortunately for them, my corny sense of humor! My parents were ecstatic to have their daughter back, and my siblings felt the same way.

In a little over a year, God had me singing in the church where He had saved me. I went from sitting in the last row crying hysterically to Him to being on stage singing joyfully to Him. If that doesn't demonstrate the transformative power of the Lord's grace, mercy, forgiveness, and love, I don't know what does. He is such a good God.

> *Praise the Lord. Praise the Lord, my soul. I will praise the Lord all my life; I will sing praise to my God as long as I live.*
>
> Psalm 146: 1-2 (NIV)

I made many friends while on the worship team, which filled my heart with happiness after so many years of loneliness. I always think back to one rehearsal in particular because I experienced a significant spiritual moment during it. I was looking around the room at my friends, and my perspective was extraordinary because it felt like I was there but not there at the same time. I felt separated, set apart, as if I was seeing things from a heavenly view, not a human one. I watched them all as they laughed and smiled while discussing the music we were singing for God. The joy in the room was effusive, and in that moment, I realized just how full my life had become. It felt like God had paused time to give me a split second of elevated awareness so I could fully appreciate all He had done in my life. Immediately, I felt tears of gratitude pool in my eyes. Then, a second later, I suddenly had a vivid flashback of my cats and drinking in my old apartment. A wave of grief hit me as I thought of them and my previous life. My tears threatened to spill over, but I blinked them away because I didn't want anyone to see me cry. It's not that I didn't want my family in Christ to see my emotions, but rather that I didn't want to explain them. It wasn't the time, it wasn't the place, and besides, I hadn't told anyone yet that I was in recovery. I frequently told myself that I didn't want anyone in church to know I was a recovering alcoholic because I was entitled to live my new life without any comparisons to my old one.

However, I eventually realized I feared criticism and judgment. I wondered if they would still love me. I questioned if they would still respect me. I feared that they might avoid me. Remnants of shame still lingered in my soul, and fear of abandonment still tugged at my heart.

The irony was that I had no trouble telling people in recovery about my God but couldn't bring myself to tell God's people about my recovery.

The Lord knew this. He knew that I was struggling with my new identity. So, He revealed the error of my ways through something that was about to happen. It was a situation that would put all of my insecurities in the spotlight.

It happened on a Sunday, at the end of our rehearsal before service. Our worship director, Kharl, said we were done and could relax before the congregation arrived.

I was about to leave the stage when one of our pastors walked up to me and said he was very happy I was singing on the worship team. He also mentioned that he knew I was in recovery and thought it was wonderful.

Absolutely nothing he said or did was wrong. Someone told my pastor I was in recovery, and he thought everyone knew. That wasn't the case, of course, but there was no way he could have known that. However, when my pastor saw the look on my face, he was immediately remorseful because he put two and two together. He realized that he wasn't supposed to know. I quickly assured him that it was fine and that I greatly appreciated his support. Then I hugged him and left the stage. As I did, I felt my anxiety rising because my sobriety was no longer a secret.

In the twelve-step programs, we are taught that we're only as sick as our secrets, so I should have known better. In retrospect, I can see that it was a sin of omission. Fear had me living a double life again, much like I did in the past. The only difference was that I was hiding my recovery instead of my addiction.

Fear and shame were threatening to ruin my life again, and the scariest part was that I didn't even realize it. I couldn't see that I needed to make peace with my past before I could face my future faithfully. My secret didn't serve me well because it prevented me from fully settling into my new identity. However, I would finally come to understand a very important truth: my past molded and shaped me, but it didn't define me. God had changed that when He changed me.

Singing during service that day is a blur to me. I can't remember much of it because my emotions were in upheaval the entire time I was on stage. I might as well have had the word alcoholic written on my forehead for everyone to see because that is exactly how exposed, vulnerable, and humiliated I felt while I was up there. We usually sing for about fifteen minutes at the beginning of service, but it felt much longer than that to me. When I left the stage, I wanted to run out of the church, but I couldn't because there were two services, and I had only sung at one. By the time I finally left the church, I was emotionally exhausted.

As I walked to my car, my chest felt tight with sorrow. I kept thinking, *Who would do this to me? Why would they do this to me?* As soon as I drove away, I began crying and continued to do so during the entire forty-five-minute drive back home.

When I walked through the door of my parents' house, they took one look at me and were immediately concerned. They asked me what was wrong and I told them what happened. Then, I mentioned that I was contemplating leaving the church. At that, my father stopped me.

He said, "You shouldn't leave the church over this; they did nothing wrong. I know you're hurt because someone didn't respect your privacy, but you have nothing to be ashamed of."

I replied, "But eventually, everyone at church will know, and I didn't want anyone to know."

Then my father said, "Why, Nina? These people seem to care about you, and your pastor said he thought it was wonderful that you're in recovery. Recovery is a huge part of your life, so you wouldn't have been able to keep it a secret for very long if you intended to stay with this church. Do you want to stay with this church?"

I paused and said, "Of course, I want to stay with this church. I love it, and I love my church family."

My father responded by saying, "Then control the narrative. Tell your story with pride and take your power back. The person who did this might have done so accidentally, but even if they did it intentionally, they will no longer have the power to hurt you if you speak your truth."

> *For whatever is hidden is meant to be disclosed, and whatever is concealed is meant to be brought out into the open.*
>
> Mark 4:22 (NIV)

From that day forward, I owned my truth and made no apologies for my recovery. Now, when I speak of my sobriety, I do so with pride and gratitude. I'm proud because I've worked very hard to better myself and my life, and I'm grateful because God has helped me with all of it.

Fortunately, what hurt me didn't hinder me. Whether that person meant to or not, they helped set me free. Yes, my hand was forced, but that pressure broke the last shackle of my shame. Truth be told, if I knew who the person was, I'd shake their hand today. Everything happened the way it did so that I could fulfill God's purpose for my life. I believe the Lord might have even orchestrated the whole situation Himself, but if He didn't, He took great care to integrate it seamlessly into the plans He had for me.

> *And we know that in all things God works for the good of those who love him, who have been called according to his purpose. For those God foreknew he also predestined to be conformed to the image of his Son, that he might be the firstborn among many brothers and sisters.*
>
> Romans 8:28–29 (NIV)

As faith would have it, I sang "Freedom" by Jesus Culture the first time I sang lead on the worship team. It was a fitting song because it perfectly described what the Lord had done in my life. I was sober for two years at that point, and everyone on the worship team knew I was in recovery. So when I sang "Freedom," I sang it with conviction because I was living my truth. I was singing of freedom from addiction and from the shame I had felt about my addiction. I was singing about my life.

That was a very special day for me because my father, Richard, and stepmother, Evelyn, came to see me sing. They sat in the front row, but as soon as the music started, they stood up with everyone else. Then they looked up at the stage and watched me sing to the Lord. Their faces were beaming with happiness and pride because I was leading worship. I was doing what I loved again, among people who loved me.

> *Now the Lord is the Spirit, and where the Spirit of the Lord is, there is freedom.*
>
> 2 Corinithians 3:17 (NIV)

By this time, much of my life was centered around my church. I even had a job right around the corner from the church. All of which meant that I was constantly on the road, driving forty-five minutes or more back and forth between church, work, and home. Eventually, I decided I wanted to move. When I informed my family about my decision, my father told me they were completely comfortable with it. Not only did I have my friends at church, but I also had friends in recovery who knew me from the beginning of my journey. So, between the two, my family knew that I had a great support system.

Before I moved, something happened that would change my life even further. The Lord would heal me again, but this time, He would do it through a blessing.

It happened while I was at work one day, at the end of a company sales meeting. My boss, Robert, looked at me and said, "I hear you're a crazy cat lady with no cat." I was so stunned by his words that I sat there, mute, for a minute while everyone around the table laughed. Before I could respond, Robert pulled out his phone and showed me a picture of a beautiful, long-haired white Persian cat. He said that her name was Chloe and that he and his wife needed a new home for her because she was scared of their other animals.

I couldn't help myself. I took his phone and stared at the picture of his cat. Almost immediately, I felt my heart ache with sorrow and regret. I told Robert that I couldn't take her because I didn't have my apartment yet and wouldn't have it for another month; then I returned his phone. However, that didn't deter him in the least.

My boss said, "That's not a problem. We just want her to have a good home. We would be willing to wait for you to move into your new place."

Smiling politely, I said, "I'm not sure I can take her, but in the worst-case scenario, I can find a home for her."

As I walked out of the conference room, I recalled Derek and Maxi's looks when I left them at the shelter. The scared look in their eyes, their confusion, and their sadness. To this day, I can still hear the way Maxi cried when I was walking out of the room, and I heard his cries again that day as I made my way to the bathroom. I needed to compose myself because I was about to cry.

Once I got to the bathroom, I allowed myself to shed a few tears, but nothing more because shame was telling me that I had no right to grieve a tragedy of my own making. Once I calmed down, I left the bathroom and headed towards my desk. When I got there, I saw a picture of Chloe taped to my computer screen. My manager had taken it upon himself to print the picture from my boss's phone. When he saw me looking at it, he said, "How can you resist that face? Look at her, she's gorgeous!" I couldn't argue with him because he was right, but it wasn't about her. It was about me. I didn't think I deserved her. Not just her, but any cat.

Later in the day, my boss, Robert, texted me a few pictures of her, and I immediately posted them on my social media page to try to find her a home. Afterward, I walked into his office to tell him I had posted her pictures on my page and reiterated that I could find someone to take her. He thanked me for my help, but as I went to leave his office, he said, "We were hoping you would take her because my wife would prefer that she gets adopted by someone we know."

Immediately, I felt conflicted because I wanted to help them, but I was still struggling with shame. Shame told me that I didn't deserve to have her because I had failed my boys. Shame told me that if they knew what I had done to Derek and Maxi, they would never give her to me. So, I replied, "We will see what happens. If no one offers to take her, I will, but I highly doubt that will happen. She is a beautiful cat. Someone will want her."

When I returned to my desk, I stared at her picture again. I tried to imagine what her personality was like and wondered who her mommy would be. Then I started praying I would find the right person to take her.

After work, while driving home, my friend Kira called to ask me about the pictures I posted. Excited, she said, "Why don't you take her, Nina? She looks like such a sweet baby!"

Kira was a friend I made through my twelve-step program, and she knew my story. She knew that I had left my baby boys at the high-kill shelter and what had become of them.

I replied, "You know why I can't take her; I don't deserve her."

Then Kira said something that meant so much to me and that I've never forgotten. She said, "Nina, that's your cat. God sent you a new baby to love. Stop trying to give her away."

I started crying and said, "She is my cat, isn't she?"

Kira replied softly, "Yes, she is. Now take down those pictures when you get home; that cat already has a mommy."

She was right; God sent me a new baby to love. He saw that shame was still in my story, just in a different place, and He wanted to eradicate it once and for all. God also knew that I would need a companion because, as dark as the world can be, it was about to get even darker. It wouldn't take me long to see how perfect His timing was once again.

In March 2020, I moved into my apartment. On my first day there, I became Chloe's mommy. My boss and his wife dropped her off and were kind enough to help me move some of my things in. When they left, it was just me, a bunch of boxes, and a tiny, fluffy new baby to love.

I don't know who was more nervous, me or Chloe. When I looked at the cat carrier on the floor, I felt my heart beating like it would come out of my chest. I heard her tiny meows coming from inside, so I unzipped the carrier and backed away slowly. Understanding cats as I did, I knew I shouldn't crowd her, so I went to the sink to wash some dishes I had unpacked.

Only a few minutes later, I looked down and saw Chloe looking up at me with her big, beautiful green eyes. Immediately, my heart melted, and I told her, "I'm your new mommy, and I'm going to take care of you."

Chloe followed me all day as I unpacked the rest of my things. She would constantly jump on or into the boxes, which slowed me down but had me laughing my way through the tedious work. I loved every minute of her silly antics and fell in love with her.

It amazes me, though not in a good way, how quickly the heart can adapt to loneliness. After a while, it can be hard to remember what life felt like before the empty spaces existed. When I had my other babies, there was a massive void in my life because I didn't have God, although I didn't realize at the time what I was missing.

Then, I had God but didn't have my babies to love, and that created a new void, a maternal one. In just one day, Chloe started to fulfill my suppressed desire to nurture and love something outside of myself.

Chloe cuddled with me when I finally got into bed later that night. You would have thought we'd lived with each other forever because the transition was seamless. We became a family almost instantly.

God gave me a magnificent blessing that he knew I needed but that I didn't think I deserved.

Unfortunately, during this time, the world was panicking over Covid. I tried my best not to give in to the fear that seemed to be spreading across the globe like wildfire. Instead, I kept praying to God for His protection. Every day, I prayed for my family, myself, and friends. I constantly tried to turn my worries over to the Lord.

However, only a week after I moved, the country was put on lockdown; we were all in quarantine. So there I was, nearly an hour away from my family, and I couldn't see my friends from church either. I was forced into isolation, which is not mentally healthy for anyone, but for a person with a substance use disorder, it is very dangerous. It didn't help that the liquor stores were still open, ready to provide people with a means of escape from the nightmare we all seemed to be living in.

Being in quarantine was challenging for me, as I know it was for many people, but I was also very lonely because it was just me and Chloe. After many years of secluding myself, I had come to love the feeling of community surrounding me at church and within my own family. However, the pandemic wasn't allowing me that comfort anymore.

Sadly, the day came when loneliness overwhelmed me completely, which had me crying and pacing in my tiny studio apartment. I felt like a caged animal. Suddenly, the old familiar feeling of not wanting to be in my skin came upon me, and not long after that, the physical ache that told me my body was craving the thing that almost killed me. Both feelings petrified me and had my heart pounding with fear.

I walked over to my bed and sat down. However, I still didn't feel safe, so I pushed myself back on my bed until my back pressed against the wall. Then, I looked across the room and saw my purse on my desk. Oddly, it felt like I was entranced by it. I couldn't seem to take my eyes off of it. It felt like there was a giant magnet in my purse that was trying to pull me toward it. The feeling was surreal. Everything inside me told me I had to get my purse, so much so that I began to lie to myself. I told myself I needed my purse because my cell phone was in it and that I needed my phone so I could call someone in recovery to ask for help. Then I told myself that no harm would come to me if I got off my bed, so I started pushing myself away from the wall but stopped abruptly. I stopped because as I visualized walking across the room to get my purse, I also saw myself grabbing it and walking right out the door to go to the liquor store.

As I mentioned earlier in my story, my former therapist, Chris, showed me how to dig deep to find the truth, no matter how uncomfortable it made me or how ugly the truth was. He taught me that I must never lie to myself. Out of all the many life-altering lessons I learned from him at the rehab, that one was the most important, especially on that day. I say that because as I sat there, I forced myself to accept a very dark and dismal truth: I wanted to drink. I didn't understand why I wanted to; I just knew I did, and that's all I needed to know.

I looked down at the floor and knew I couldn't step on it. Intuitively, I knew that would be the end of my sobriety. So, I did what many in Scripture did before me when faced with a foe they couldn't defeat; I turned my battle over to the Lord. Through my tears, I called out to God and begged Him to help me. I asked the Lord to save me, and He heard me. I knew He did when something inside told me to go to sleep. It was the Holy Spirit.

When I received His response, I yelled, "I'm not tired!"

Then, I hit my bed in frustration and cried even harder. After my outburst, I heard the same answer, "Go to sleep."

Feeling defeated and frustrated beyond belief, I laid down. I don't think my head was even on the pillow for more than a few minutes before I fell into a deep sleep.

> *But you, Lord, are a shield around me, my glory, the One who lifts my head high. I call out to the Lord, and he answers me from his holy mountain. I lie down and sleep; I wake again, because the Lord sustains me.*
>
> Psalm 3:3-5 (NIV)

When I woke up, I looked at the window above my front door and saw it was dark, which confused me. Then I looked at my clock and saw that five hours had passed, which shocked me. I didn't understand how I slept that long when I hadn't even been tired. However, what stunned me the most was that I didn't want to drink. I no longer felt the physical craving; I no longer felt mentally tortured; I was fine. I felt at peace. I looked at the floor, and it didn't scare me anymore. I knew I could get up and walk around because I was in no danger of drinking. The Lord healed me while I slept. Everything that had been disturbing my heart and soul was gone; He completely restored me. Then, it dawned on me that the rest I needed was spiritual, not physical.

Finally, I got out of bed. When I stood up, I found myself staring at my feet and the floor as if I were seeing both for the first time. I started to cry again, but my tears were of joy and gratitude. I thanked the Lord profusely for His protection.

Throughout that entire ordeal, it felt like I was fighting far more than just my addiction. If I had lost that battle, I would have lost the war for my life, but instead, the Lord declared victory for me as I slept.

> *Put on the full armor of God, so that you can take your stand against the devil's schemes. For our struggle is not against flesh and blood, but against the rulers, against the authorities, against the powers of this dark world and against the spiritual forces of evil in the heavenly realms. Therefore put on the full armor of God, so that when the day of evil comes, you may be able to stand your ground, and after you have done everything, to stand.*
>
> Ephesians 6:11-13 (NIV)

I had dedicated my life to the Lord while I was in rehab, but after my near relapse, I was even more devoted, which I didn't think was possible. That experience inspired me to spend even more time with Him, and I soon discovered that I still had much more to give and give up. God showed me where I was falling short, which He will always do if you ask Him to reveal such things. However, don't be surprised if the Lord shines His light on the things within you that you don't want to see. I say that because that's exactly what happened to me.

Since childhood, my greatest desire has been to be a wife and mother. Perhaps other people view success and fulfillment differently, but I desired those things above all others. My aspirations never involved business or financial wealth; my greatest dream was always of family.

I wanted a man to love, one I could love with all of me, sparing nothing. I longed for a man who would love me completely. One who would laugh at my silliness and comfort me when I cried, who would hold and protect me when the world felt like it would break me. I wanted a man who would understand my heart and soul, and I wanted that man to be my husband.

I also wanted to have his children, to be a mother. I wanted to pour my love into our babies and help them discover who they were meant to be. I wanted to tuck our children into bed at night and give them butterfly kisses on their cheeks like my mother had when I was a child. I wanted to devote my life to my husband and children. That was my dream, but obviously, it never came to fruition.

I was responsible for the death of my dream. There was no way I could have had the life I imagined with the broken concepts I had of love and self. For all those years, I had no idea what love truly was. I didn't know what it felt like or how it behaved, and that isn't meant to be an affront to anyone else; it's simply a spiritual statement of fact about myself. It was reflected in who I was, who I chose, and what I did.

When I finally got sober, I thought that would be one of the first blessings that the Lord would bestow upon me. When it wasn't, it upset me greatly because I felt I deserved that type of love, especially after waiting so many years. Unfortunately, I was emotionally fixated on getting the one thing I never had rather than appreciating all the things God had given me back.

I began to think it might be the only thing that could make me relapse. I even told my sponsor that when she asked me what my downfall could be. I told her, "If God doesn't send me the man I've been waiting for my whole life, I don't know if I will want to stay sober."

After I said that, she looked at me with shock and disappointment and said, "Wow, I didn't expect that. I'll get back to you in a few months to see what you think then."

Sure enough, she did ask me again and even again after that, but my answer was always the same.

The Lord shined a light on my bitterness and entitlement. It was the ugliness I didn't want to see. It was sinfulness that required correction from my creator because I couldn't rectify it myself. Through the Holy Spirit, I heard, "Am I not enough for you? Would you throw away the life I gave back to you because you don't have those things?" The guilt I felt afterward was overwhelming, and I started crying hysterically. The Lord rebuked me, and I immediately repented, begging for His forgiveness.

It took me a while to calm down, but once I did, I had a revelation. God's will had given me life, saved my life, and brought me back to life, while my own will always brought death to my doorstep. How could I think for a second that my ways were better than His? I mentally berated myself for my lack of gratitude because I dared to complain about the life He so graciously gave back to me. I wouldn't even be alive were it not for my Lord and Savior! I was ashamed of my audacity. The blessings He had bestowed upon me during my sobriety were bountiful and beautiful, but my atrocious attitude didn't reflect that. I'm beyond thankful that God was both merciful and gracious enough to provide spiritual lessons that forever changed me.

> *Endure hardship as discipline; God is treating you as his children. For what children are not disciplined by their father? If you are not disciplined—and everyone undergoes discipline—then you are not legitimate, not true sons and daughters at all. No discipline seems pleasant at the time, but painful. Later on, however, it produces a harvest of righteousness and peace for those who have been trained by it.*
>
> Hebrews 12:7-8, 11 (NIV)

That was the day I learned that I had to stop fighting the narrative of my story when it didn't align with my expectations. It only fueled negative emotions that tainted my soul and weakened my spirit.

Humility always reminds me that the role I play is never more important than God's. It is easy to walk with the Lord when things are going well or as I want them to. However, mature faith, faith at its fullest, requires that I walk with Him even when the journey is laborious and I'm unsure of my destination. I must remember that His vision for my life is eternal, while mine is temporal.

Marriage might never be part of my story, and the Lord's loving lessons prompted me to make peace with that possibility. Of course, I hope that's not the case, but only time will tell, and when it does, I will accept the Lord's will for my life on the matter.

I finally realized that my life as a child and follower of Christ is not mine; it's His. I'm but a thread in His tapestry of the world and all the lives within it. Only God gives the thread its color, meaning, placement, and purpose.

I might not understand His ways, but I can always hold on to hope because He is such a good God.

> *Whoever tries to keep their life will lose it, and whoever loses their life will preserve it.*
>
> Luke 17:33 (NIV)

A couple of months later, I received an email from my former therapist, Christopher Michael Burns, LCSW, CSAT, informing me of a new serving opportunity at the church.

Chris has been a staff member with theCross since 2015. He is the healing minister at our church but is also referred to as one of our pastors because he is highly regarded.

In the email, Chris told me that he was creating a healing ministry called Care and Recovery Night that would be held on Friday nights from 6:00 pm to 8:00 pm at the church. Then, he went on to explain his vision. During the first hour of the evening, Chris would deliver a sermon, and every week, he would cover a different topic. Afterward, in the second hour, he would have the people who attended split into gender-specific support groups: one for people in recovery and one for those who weren't.

At the end of the email, Chris asked if I would be interested in being a leader for the women's recovery support group.

When I read about his vision, I couldn't have been more impressed because it was precisely what the community needed, and when I read his request that I will be a leader for women in recovery, I was overwhelmed with gratitude. I immediately thanked Chris for the opportunity and said I would love to serve in that capacity.

Care and Recovery Night was launched in September of 2020. God's timing was perfect yet again because the ongoing pandemic was causing severe physical, emotional, and spiritual trauma.

When I first walked into the room where Care and Recovery Night would be held, I was amazed by the beautiful space that Chris and his wife created. Chris's wife is not part of the staff at the church, but she assisted her husband in creating a beautiful environment and atmosphere for the ministry. It was obviously a labor of love for both of them.

As I looked around, I saw the stage where Chris would preach. On it was a podium with a chair where he could sit while delivering his sermons. There were also candles illuminating both sides of the stage, creating a soft, warm glow, and on the wall behind the stage, there was a stunning wooden cross. The space they had created was inviting, comforting, and peaceful. It was perfect.

Our first night went off without a hitch, although few people were in attendance. However, we expected that. For months on end, everyone had been told that isolation was crucial for survival and that community was a death sentence.

We needed to let go of the unhealthy habits we developed. We needed a safe and sacred space where we could openly discuss how we felt about everything that was transpiring. The media was bombarding us with news and images of death and devastation on a daily basis, making it almost impossible not to ingest hopelessness and despair.

For far too long, most of our conversations had been centered around sickness and suffering. It's not that there's anything wrong with discussing things that have wounded us, but it is unhealthy if that remains the only topic of conversation.

The purpose of the ministry is to recover from past and present traumas, no matter what they are. We focus on how our Lord and Savior, Jesus Christ, can offer us peace amongst chaos and healing after we've been hurt.

The ministry's motto has always been: Come for the hope, stay for the healing.

As the weeks moved on, attendance increased. Slowly but surely, we were establishing a new culture where people could discuss their mental, spiritual, and emotional health without fear of judgment or shame.

> *Do not conform to the pattern of this world, but be transformed by the renewing of your mind. Then you will be able to test and approve what God's will is—his good, pleasing and perfect will.*
>
> Romans 12:2 (NIV)

In March of 2021, Chris asked if I would do a sermon at the ministry. I was honored that he would entrust me with something so important, but I was petrified at the thought of speaking in public, especially because I would be preaching the gospel. Despite my many fears, I agreed to do it because I was excited to serve God in a way I had never imagined. Chris also made a suggestion regarding the message I would deliver; he thought I should use a devotional I had written for the women's ministry and elaborate on it.

A few months prior, Linda Crossman, the women's ministry director, asked me to write a devotional about spiritual growth. It was the first one I ever wrote, and it was an enlightening experience.

As I mentioned earlier, I first met Linda when I auditioned for the worship team. Over the years, we became good friends while serving on the team together. I was very forthcoming with Linda about my life in recovery and my prior life in active addiction. She knew my story very well. However, that didn't stop me from being pleasantly surprised when she offered me such a wonderful opportunity.

As I wrote the sermon for ministry, I was sure to include parts of my devotional, just as Chris had asked me to. In fact, that's when I realized the Lord had called me to worship Him through the written word again. God seemed to be using my voice in a different way. He wanted me to sing His praises on paper, not just a microphone.

Writing the message was challenging, but the thought of preaching the gospel while being on stage was daunting. I didn't feel equipped to lead in that way, but I knew if the Lord wanted me to serve in that capacity, He would also make me capable.

The night finally came to deliver my sermon on spiritual growth, and I was a nervous wreck. I kept walking around the ministry looking for things to do, but all the volunteers had everything covered. They didn't need any help, but I did, and that's when I knew what I needed to do.

I went to the bathroom to get away from anyone for a few minutes and prayed. I asked the Lord to help me. I asked Him to give me the peace that only He can give, the one that transcends all understanding. Afterward, I left the bathroom, and that's when I saw our lead pastor, Mark Crossman, walk into the ministry.

I was shocked. I had no idea that he would be there.

I walked over to Pastor Mark and hugged him. Then, I said, "What are you doing here?"

He smiled and responded, "I came to see you do your first message at the ministry. I wasn't going to miss it!"

We chatted a little more, and I thanked him for coming. Then I walked to the stage. As I stepped up and onto it, I could feel my legs starting to shake, like they always do when I'm really nervous. So, I quickly walked over to the podium and sat down on the chair behind it.

A few minutes later, I began delivering the sermon. When I first started speaking, my voice quivered slightly. However, as I continued on, it eventually stopped because I focused on what I was there to do rather than who was there.

There were parts of my sermon that made me cry. I couldn't help it. It was difficult to remain composed when I was discussing how the Lord had saved me and what He saved me from. I was speaking about spiritual growth but referencing my personal experiences with it, so I was highly emotional.

Finally, I reached the end of my message. I was so relieved. I had faced my fears and done what the Lord had called me to do. I was obedient, even though I felt overwhelmed by the responsibility He had given me.

I started to gather up the papers I had on the podium, the ones I had printed my sermon on. Then, I looked up and saw that Pastor Mark was walking over to me with a huge smile on his face. Immediately, my relief turned to joy because my pastor looked proud of me.

Before I knew it, we were hugging again, and he said, "Nina, you were phenomenal! Are you trying to take my job?"

Then Pastor Mark started laughing, and so did I. Quickly, I replied, "Absolutely not!"

It meant so much to me that he came to support me that night, although I must admit that it was quite intimidating to do a sermon in front of my pastor.

Pastor Mark Crossman became our lead pastor in August 2020, right in the middle of the pandemic. He had to lead our church through an unprecedented time, and did so with enormous strength and grace. I respect him and his wife, Linda, immensely. They have both supported me incredibly throughout the years. I'm exceedingly blessed to have them in my life.

I can say the same about our healing minister, Chris Burns. He helped me tremendously, both in my walk in recovery and in Christ. Chris always pushed me to do more than I thought I could, and the sermon was a perfect example of that. Where I saw limitations, Chris showed me possibilities.

Every spiritual gift I have was either inspired, encouraged, or cultivated by staff members of my church. I consider them family and love them all dearly. I wouldn't be the woman of Christ I am today without their steadfast love and support.

> *Therefore encourage one another and build each other up, just as in fact you are doing.*
>
> 1 Thessalonians 5:11 (NIV)

As I continued to walk with God, He continued to expand the ways I would serve, which is how He amazed me yet again. My Lord and Savior provided me with an incredible opportunity that I never saw coming.

It happened towards the latter part of 2022 when I received an email from our executive pastor, Jacob Baumann. In it, he asked if I would be interested in serving on the board of directors. To say that I was stunned would be an understatement. I read the email twice to be certain that I hadn't misunderstood what he wrote. Then, I quickly replied that I would love to.

The first time I attended theCross was in November of 2017. I hadn't even been in rehab for a full week when I walked into the church. I was no more than a shell of a woman. I cried hysterically through my first service but knew I had found my church by the time I left. I knew it because God made it clear that He was with me on that day. However, there was no way I could have possibly imagined what my Messiah had in store for me.

Exactly five years later, in November of 2022, I was elected to the board of directors at theCross.

Serving on the board has been such a wonderful experience. It is an honor and privilege to represent my brothers and sisters in Christ.

> *"For I know the plans I have for you," declares the Lord, "plans to prosper you and not to harm you, plans to give you hope and a future."*
>
> Jeremiah 29:11

While I no longer serve in the ministry, I will always treasure the time I had there. To this day, it continues to grow and thrive; however, it is now called Restoration Nights. Our healing minister, Chris Burns, also changed how the support groups were conducted. They are still gender-specific, but there is no longer one group for people in recovery and another for those who aren't. Now, everyone is recovering from this broken world together.

For most of my life, I wondered why I had to endure so much pain. I walked with many wounds for a very long time. Some of them were inflicted by others, but I also inflicted wounds on myself. Looking back now, I realize that I might have started out as a victim, but I didn't remain there; eventually, I became a volunteer.

> *Now a man who was lame from birth was being carried to the temple gate called Beautiful, where he was put every day to beg from those going into the temple courts. When he saw Peter and John about to enter, he asked them for money. Peter looked straight at him, as did John. Then Peter said, "Look at us!" So the man gave them his attention, expecting to get something from them. Then Peter said, "Silver or gold I do not have,*

> *but what I do have I give you. In the name of Jesus Christ of Nazareth, walk." Taking him by the right hand, he helped him up, and instantly the man's feet and ankles became strong. He jumped to his feet and began to walk. Then he went with them into the temple courts, walking and jumping, and praising God. When all the people saw him walking and praising God, they recognized him as the same man who used to sit begging at the temple gate called Beautiful, and they were filled with wonder and amazement at what had happened to him. When Peter saw this, he said to them: "Fellow Israelites, why does this surprise you? Why do you stare at us as if by our own power or godliness we had made this man walk? The God of Abraham, Isaac and Jacob, the God of our fathers, has glorified his servant Jesus. You handed him over to be killed, and you disowned him before Pilate, though he had decided to let him go. You disowned the Holy and Righteous One and asked that a murderer be released to you. You killed the author of life, but God raised him from the dead. We are witnesses of this. By faith in the name of Jesus, this man whom you see and know was made strong. It is Jesus' name and the faith that comes through him that has completely healed him, as you can all see.*
>
> Acts 3:2-10, 12-16 (NIV)

Jesus has healed so many of my wounds during my recovery journey. Though, to be clear, my recovery wasn't just from addiction; it was also from trauma, depression, anxiety, and loss. Faith set me free from the bondage of grief because I finally realized that my creator was the only one who could heal my broken heart and wounded soul.

At the ministry, the Lord used every part of my story. He used the life I lived before He saved me and my life with Him afterward. Over the years, I drew from my painful past many times while leading the women's support groups, but I also explained how the Lord loved me back to life. I related to their suffering but always reminded them that there was hope for healing in the future.

Pain is a very bitter pill until it serves a purpose, but once it does, sweetness surrounds it like honey, making it easier to swallow. Knowing what hurt me can help others make sense of the seemingly senseless. It is the blessing after the burden.

> *And we know that in all things God works for the good of those who love him, who have been called according to his purpose.*
>
> Romans 8:28 (NIV)

Serving in the ministry was one of the greatest joys of my life, but I also experienced substantial spiritual growth from it in my relationship with Christ, so I will always be eternally grateful for my time there.

Leading the women's support groups made me realize I had more work to do as a Christian woman. I quickly discovered that I would need to be well-versed in scripture if I was going to lead others effectively.

I knew Jesus was the answer to every problem we face because I had experienced it personally. However, to minister to my sisters in Christ well, I needed more than that. So, I decided to read the Bible in its entirety, which I had never done before.

That was life-changing because I learned so much more about God and myself through Scripture. It is, without a doubt, the greatest tool I have in my journey as a woman in recovery and in Christ. To this day, I find myself in the Word almost every day.

I ministered to women, but they also ministered to me. I shared many personal things with my sisters in Christ in the support groups. We all learned from each other and supported one another, and it was all done with great love.

One of the many things I always loved about the ministry is that it's open to everyone, not just our church family. I met many women who attended our church, but also many who didn't. Some knew Christ their whole lives, while others were meeting Him for the first time. That is the beauty of community; it doesn't matter where we are on our walk with the Lord; the only thing that matters is that we are walking together.

> *And let us consider how we may spur one another on toward love and good deeds, not giving up meeting together, as some are in the habit of doing, but encouraging one another—and all the more as you see the Day approaching.*
>
> Hebrews 10:24-25 (NIV)

After that initial sermon, I proceeded to do more at the ministry when asked, which was usually once every season. To this day, I still go back from time to time to preach a message of hope and healing, and I enjoy it immensely. However, before I ever deliver a sermon in front of my church family, I always send a copy to my stepsister Lisa to get her feedback.

Lisa also makes me feel invincible, and that's precisely how I needed to feel before I delivered the last message I did because it was essentially my testimony in a condensed format.

I had to touch on very dark parts of my story because I was discussing how we can feel joy after sorrow and drew from my own experiences. At one point, I even got so choked up that I had to pause for a couple of minutes to compose myself; however, I continued on.

Delivering that message took a lot out of me, yet the same can be said about writing this book. It was exceedingly difficult to revisit so many painful parts of my journey, but it was necessary. I had to thoroughly explain the magnitude of my misery to convey the Lord's miraculous work in my life properly.

The beautiful life I live now was born of pain, but there is no testimony without a test. As a child, I was taught the truth of the gospel through scripture, but as an adult, I have lived it.

> *They triumphed over him by the blood of the Lamb and by the word of their testimony; they did not love their lives so much as to shrink from death.*
>
> Revelation 12:11 (NIV)

The ministry has evolved since its inception, and so did the ways I served there. A worship team was created for Restoration Nights, so I also sang there from time to time.

My favorite song is "Defender" because it perfectly depicts what God has done and continues to do in my life. I get emotional every time I sing it because it is my love song to the Lord.

I especially connect with the lines: "When I thought I lost me, you knew where I left me. You reintroduced me to your love. You picked up all my pieces and put me back together. You are the Defender of my heart."

The lyrics are perfect because I had lost myself along the way, and if God hadn't saved me, I never would have found myself again. The Lord also took the fragmented pieces of my heart and soul and put them back together. He made me whole.

Then, of course, my Savior went even further because Christ will never leave you where you are or as you are. Through His sovereignty, He transformed me.

As a new creation in Christ, I don't think the same or behave the same, which is as it should be. My soul is no longer saturated with sorrow. Instead, most days, it's filled with laughter and joy.

> *Therefore, if anyone is in Christ, the new creation has come: The old has gone, the new is here!*
>
> 2 Corinthians 5:17 (NIV)

There are four stages in the evolution process of a caterpillar becoming a butterfly. However, before the new creation can emerge, there is an extremely painful process. During the third stage, the caterpillar must break itself down completely. Then, and only then, can it reorganize itself into a new form.

Such is our transformation in recovery and in Christ. In recovery, we call it hitting our bottom. It is when we finally come to realize that we can no longer continue as we have been, as who we have been, when the pain of remaining the same far outweighs our fear of change.

The same can be said of people who don't struggle with addiction issues. Their lives can be in turmoil simply because living in their own will has been detrimental to them. Or perhaps they have also suffered traumas and need the infinite grace, love, and mercy of Christ to heal them and make them new again. The parallels are there if one wishes to see them.

To achieve greatness, I'm referring to restoration and transformation of the heart, mind and soul, we must evolve. We must change. Often, prior to such a miraculous and divine change, we need to be broken down, for it is only when we look at the fragmented pieces of ourselves and our lives that we finally surrender. When there is no fight left in us and our arrogance has run dry, we learn humility. That is when God does His best work in us, when we are no longer in our own way.

So it was with me. I was entirely broken down when I walked into that rehab at forty-four years old. I felt like I was shattered into a thousand tiny shards of glass, all of which were cutting me and anyone else I came into close contact with. I felt all the broken pieces in me intensely and the desolate void that surrounded them as well. Emotionally, it was excruciating, but it was necessary. It was the precursor to my rebirth, my Chrysalis in Christ.

Then, just as the butterfly's beauty can not be ignored and it is able to soar, such was my transformation in Christ. I speak not of physical beauty but of the radiant spiritual light I shine in the world because it is the light of my Lord and Savior. I speak of soaring because His love for me has brought me to new heights and achievements.

I finally became a butterfly.

Afterword

He said to her, "Daughter, your faith has healed you. Go in peace and be freed from your suffering.

Mark 5:34 (NIV)

Jesus saved me from a life of alcoholism and trauma, but you might be struggling with something completely different. There is no need to worry if you are because God's love heals all wounds. The Lord knew every battle you would ever face in your lifetime before the very beginning of time, so you can rest assured that our Savior already has His rescue plan for you in place.

You, my sister in Christ, were born to be a butterfly.

About the Author

Nina Pajonas is an aspiring Christian author with a deep passion for writing and women's ministry.

In 2020, during the pandemic, she helped to build and grow a healing ministry within her church that is still thriving today. Over the years, she has ministered to many women by drawing from her own experiences with addiction and trauma and her recovery from both.

From Broken to Butterfly is her debut book and memoir.

You can find her on Facebook, Instagram, and her website: www.NinaPajonas.com

Printed in the USA
CPSIA information can be obtained
at www.ICGtesting.com
LVHW020521111224
798845LV00001B/154